CRIME LAB 101

CRIME LAB 101
Experimenting with Crime Detection

Robert Gardner

Walker and Company
New York

First published in the United States of America in 1992
by Walker Publishing Company, Inc.

Published simultaneously in Canada by Thomas Allen & Son
Canada, Limited, Markham, Ontario

Library of Congress Cataloging-in-Publication Data
Gardner, Robert, 1929–
Crime lab 101: experimenting with crime
detection / Robert Gardner.
p.   cm.
Includes bibliographical references (p.   ) and index.
Summary: Introduces techniques of criminal investigation,
including fingerprint and voice pattern examination, handwriting
analysis, and ballistics, and discusses the development
of forensic science.
ISBN 0-8027-8158-6 (cloth). —ISBN 0-8027-8159-4 (reinforced)
1. Criminal investigation—Juvenile literature.   [1. Criminal
investigation.]   I. Title.   II. Title: Crime lab one hundred one.
HV8073.8.G38   1992
363.2'5—dc20   92-3999
CIP
AC

Printed in the United States of America

1   2   3   4   5   6   7   8   9   10

Contents

Contents

INTRODUCTION

In this book you'll see how science and technology have helped law-enforcement agencies solve crimes. You'll learn some of the techniques of forensic science and test your own ingenuity in solving some "crimes" in your own home or school. You'll learn how to record and lift fingerprints, how to identify the ink found on a ransom note, how to find messages on a blank sheet of paper, and how to use other techniques practiced by professional crime detectors.

Activities in this book are of two kinds: The "Crime Labs" generally enable you to practice specific techniques of forensic science. The "Crime Lab Exercises," on the other hand, more closely resemble pure science experiments. They give you a chance to explore some of the principles behind the methods of detection.

In addition to having many opportunities to experiment with forensic science techniques, you'll also learn about some famous crimes and how they were or weren't solved. But more important, by using your crime-detecting skills, you'll learn how to think more clearly and effectively, abilities that will help you in whatever you do.

CRIME LAB 101

SCIENCE
AND
CRIME

$\left(\text{A}\right)$ group of hunters, hiding in woods and thickets, waited for deer to appear within their gun sights. Suddenly, one of the hunters, Robert Perry, spied an approaching deer and fired. To his dismay, a fellow hunter, not the deer, fell in the nearby brush. The bullet had killed him. In the course of the investigation that followed, the local sheriff persuaded the guilt-ridden and confused hunter to sign a confession of negligent homicide. Perry was certain that he had seen and fired at a deer, but he could not explain how the bullet had hit his friend. The sheriff, on the other hand, believed Perry to be an overzealous hunter who had caught a glimpse of what he *thought* was a deer and had fired instead at his friend.

Perry's lawyer believed that his client was innocent. However, lacking the evidence needed to convince a jury, he turned to Herbert Leon MacDonell, a well-known *criminalist*—someone who uses scientific techniques to investigate crimes. (He could have been called a forensic scientist as well—one who applies science to matters of law.) MacDonell asked to examine the gun and the fatal bullet. He noticed that the wadding, the paper used to pack the gunpowder firmly into the cartridge, was still attached to the slug that had killed the hunter. Normally, air rushing over the speeding bullet causes the wadding to fall off the bullet about two feet from the gun. Yet, the fatal bullet had traveled several hundred feet, which suggested that it had not moved fast enough for air to tear the wadding off. He also found small pieces of wood on the slug, and careful weighings revealed that about forty-five grains (nearly 14 percent) of the lead normally found in such a slug was missing.

MacDonell then conducted some tests. First, he fired Perry's gun a number of times and found that the wadding did indeed fall from the slug a short distance from the gun. Next, he visited the site where the shooting had taken place. There he found a mark on a tree trunk close to the point where the gun had been fired. The wood fibers found on the slug were similar to fibers taken from the scarred tree.

In testimony given at the trial, MacDonell argued that the slug, intended for the deer, had ricocheted off the marked tree, where it lost its high velocity, changed its direction, then struck the victim. How else could one explain the wood fibers on the slug, the attached wadding, and the fact that the mass of the slug was forty-five grains less than normal? The jury agreed. They found Perry not guilty.

In another case, MacDonell was asked to examine evidence used by a prosecuting attorney to convict another defendant. The evidence consisted of a fingerprint on an envelope that had contained a coin taken from the room of the victim. A fingerprint expert hired by the prosecutor had claimed that the print on the envelope came from the accused's thumb. MacDonell showed that the print came from a finger, not a thumb, and that a scar evident in the print could not be found on any of the defendant's fingers. When an FBI expert agreed with MacDonell's analysis, the convicted man was released.

These two instances illustrate how forensic science—the science and scientific techniques used in solving crimes—can be used to demonstrate (1) the innocence of a person being prosecuted and (2) the innocence of an innocent person. More commonly, however, forensic science is used to convince a judge or jury that a person *is* guilty of a crime. For example, during a robbery, a tank containing goldfish was knocked off a table onto the floor, where it smashed into thousands of pieces. Later, a suspect was arrested, but he denied any knowledge of the crime. However, crime-lab scientists found on his trousers tiny pieces of glass that matched the glass in the broken fish tank. Furthermore, they found fish scales on his shoes—scales that matched those of the goldfish that had been in the tank. Faced with this evidence, the man confessed to the crime.

THE BASIC PRINCIPLE OF FORENSIC SCIENCE

The basic principle of forensic science is that *a criminal always takes something to the scene of a crime and always leaves something there.* It may be a fingerprint, a footprint, a hair, fibers from his or her clothing, a note, a bullet shell, a weapon, or something else. It is the forensic scientist's job to find this evidence, compare it with similar material or substances, trace it to its origin, and then use all the evidence to reconstruct the crime.

Forensic scientists include chemists, dentists, toxicologists, pathologists, psychologists, machinists, anthropologists, and engineers, as well as detectives and the police. These experts try to identify blood, hair, fibers, glass, paint, soil, plastics, fingerprints, footprints, firearms, tool markings, documents, drugs, and other bits of evidence that police and detectives may find at the scene of a crime.

Often the evidence is so convincing that the guilty person will confess. Fingerprints found on a murder weapon may leave little doubt as to who is guilty. Sometimes, however, a lengthy investigation is necessary. In a case involving a woman found dead on the ground 200 feet below her apartment balcony, police were uncertain as to whether she had fallen, jumped, or been thrown. Neighbors thought she had committed suicide. Her husband, the beneficiary of the victim's life insurance policy, claimed that she had fallen while trying to adjust the air conditioner. After carrying out a series of tests in which dummies were dropped and pushed from the balcony, the police determined that if the woman had fallen, her body would not have been more than 10½ feet from the wall of the building. Because her body was actually found nearly 17 feet from the wall, police decided that she had been thrown or pushed from the balcony. When this evidence was presented to the husband, he confessed that he had pushed his wife to her death.

THE TOOLS OF AN AMATEUR CRIME DETECTOR

As an amateur crime detector, you will need special tools and materials to do your work. Fortunately, most of these items are inexpensive and easy to obtain. As you begin your work in crime detection, you might find it useful to organize a crime-detection kit. Following are the materials to keep in this kit:

Materials for crime-detection kit

magnifying glass

microscope and glass
  microscope slides
  (optional)

forceps

a feather or cotton

talcum powder

wide plastic sticky tape

soft pencils

paper

Superglue

ninhydrin powder
  (available in school
  laboratories or science
  supply houses)

several sheets of blotter
  paper

graduated cylinder or
  measuring cup with
  metric units

camera (optional)

THE DEVELOPMENT OF FORENSIC SCIENCE AND MODERN CRIME DETECTION

(A) rchimedes was probably the first forensic scientist. According to legend, King Heiron had commissioned a local goldsmith to make a crown of gold that the king might wear on special occasions. The king, after receiving the crown, suspected that he had been cheated, so he asked Archimedes to find out whether the crown was really made of pure gold. Archimedes thought long and hard about how he could fulfill the king's request without damaging the expensive crown. One day, while bathing, he noticed that the water level rose as he lowered his body into the tub. Suddenly, in a flash, he saw the answer to the puzzle. As legend has it, Archimedes leaped from his tub and ran naked through the streets of Syracuse, Sicily, shouting, "Eureka! Eureka!" ("I've got it! I've got it!")

Archimedes had suddenly *seen* that the volume of the crown could be measured by one's placing it in water. The crown would displace its own volume in water. At that moment, Archimedes realized that he could weigh a volume of gold equal to the volume of the crown. If the gold weighed the same as the crown, the crown was pure gold. But if it weighed less than the crown, it had been made of a lighter metal and covered with gold. When he weighed the crown, he found it was lighter than an equal volume of gold. Faced with the evidence, the goldsmith admitted he had mixed silver with gold in making the crown.

THE DEVELOPMENT OF FORENSIC SCIENCE

Sherlock Holmes, the famous fictional detective in Sir Arthur Conan Doyle's stories, was often depicted in a chemistry laboratory, test tube in hand, analyzing blood, soil, poisons, or other evidence found at the scene of a crime. Many say that Doyle anticipated the use of science in solving crimes. Whether the stories of Sherlock Holmes, written in the late nineteenth century, had any effect on the development of forensic science is subject to debate. But it was shortly after Doyle's works were published that forensic science began to play an important role in crime detection.

In 1892, Sir Francis Galton demonstrated that fingerprints are unique and do not change with age. Before Galton's study, professional police forces, such as that of Scotland Yard in England, had used the Bertillon system to identify criminals. This system consisted of a photograph of the criminal as well as 11 body measurements that included the dimensions of the head; height; and the length of the arms, legs, and feet. Alphonse Bertillon, who had devised the system, showed that the chance of two people being identical for these 11 measurements was 1 in 286,435,456. The measurements were tedious to make, however, and in 1894 Scotland Yard, recognizing the simplicity and uniqueness of fingerprints, modified the Bertillon system to include them.

In 1896, Argentina became the first nation to adopt fingerprint identification as the official means of identifying criminals. Juan Vucetich, a Buenos Aires detective, found fingerprints valuable in solving a murder in 1892. The mother of two children who had been murdered accused a neighbor of the crime. The bloody fingerprints that Vucetich found on a door frame matched the mother's fingerprints perfectly. Faced with such evidence, the mother confessed that she had killed her own children. The experience convinced Vucetich that fingerprints could play an important role in crime detection.

In 1904, the New York City police department began fingerprinting people they arrested, and the practice began spreading to other police departments throughout the country.

In France in 1910, Edmond Locard established the world's first crime laboratory. There, scientists analyzed evidence collected by police and detectives in an effort to identify the persons who had committed various crimes.

Locard's work made crime investigators aware of the need for a scientific approach to collecting and analyzing evidence found at the scene of a crime. During the 1920s, forensic laboratories were established throughout Europe. The first American crime lab was opened in Los Angeles in 1923. A second crime laboratory was established at Northwestern University six years later, but not until the 1930s was a federal crime lab opened.

J. Edgar Hoover, the director of the Bureau of Investigation, was intent on creating an efficiently run, truly professional law-enforcement agency. He hired educated, highly trained people to serve as agents. In 1932, he sought the advice of numerous scientific experts before establishing and training a staff to operate the Federal Crime Laboratory, which opened on November 24, 1932. In its first week, the lab acted on twenty cases. Today, it carries out thousands of analyses each week for FBI agents and for police departments throughout the nation. In 1935, Hoover founded the National Police Academy, an institution dedicated to training law-enforcement personnel who would know how to make good use of the Federal Crime Laboratory.

It is true that J. Edgar Hoover was overly zealous throughout his career in pursuing and trying to expose those whom he often incorrectly labeled as traitors or communists. This was especially true during the "Red scare" following World War II.

However, it was Hoover who led the movement to make law-enforcement agencies truly professional. The success and effectiveness of the Federal Crime Laboratory made it clear that science and technology would play an increasingly important role in crime detection and law enforcement. Today, for example, the FBI has more than 80 million fingerprints on file.

SCIENCE AND CRIME TODAY

Forensic science has made giant strides since Hoover established the Federal Crime Laboratory. Today there are about 400 crime laboratories and nearly 40,000 forensic scientists in the United States. The special microscopes found in some of these labs can magnify particles found at the scene of a crime by as much as 200,000 times. Modern techniques involving very sophisticated machines and procedures help forensic scientists to separate and identify chemicals found in complex mixtures. This enables them to determine the source of fibers, glass particles, paint chips, and other physical evidence collected by crime investigators. With other techniques, forensic scientists can identify bloodstains and determine their source. Portable lasers reveal fingerprints that would otherwise have gone undetected, while new chemicals and techniques enable detectives to dust and lift faint fingerprints. In addition, computer technology has speeded up and improved analysis and data retrieval, making possible also the ability to store vast amounts of information about criminals—information that can be readily exchanged within and between police departments.

Despite all the sophisticated equipment and techniques used to analyze evidence in crime labs, basic police work depends still on keen thinking, careful questioning, and detailed collection of evidence that may later find its way to a crime lab. The equipment used by the police and detectives who do this basic work is not necessarily complex or sophisticated. Much of it can be found in your own home. It is just such equipment that you will use in your own crime-detection activities.

THREE

Fingerprints and Other Prints: Something Criminals Often Leave Behind

I n keeping with the forensic scientist's basic principle, criminals bring their fingers to the scene of a crime. Fortunately for crime detectors, many criminals leave their fingerprints behind.

Each of us is born with a distinctive set of tiny ridges in the skin covering the last digit of each finger—the part of the finger on the side opposite the nail. If you look at your fingers in strong light, you can see these fine ridges quite clearly. The pattern of ridges found on your fingers persists throughout your life. Even if the skin is removed, the ridges grow back in the same pattern. Along these ridges are thousands of sweat pores. The sweat carries some of the body oils normally found on fingers, leaving an outline of the ridge pattern. Even clean hands have enough body oil to leave at least faint fingerprints. You can see, then, why many criminals wear gloves.

Fingerprints can be used to identify people found dead as a result of accident, war, murder, or other causes; to identify amnesia victims; and to identify babies in the event that they are switched in a hospital or kidnapped. Recently, fingerprints have been used by security-minded companies in place of passwords, I.D. numbers, badges, and photographs. An employee seeking entrance through a security door may press his or her thumb against a glass plate. Laser light is reflected from the finger ridges to a photoreceptor. A computer then compares the pattern against those registered in its memory. If there is no match, an alarm is sounded.

In Crime Lab 1, you'll learn how to make fingerprint records of your family members and friends. Then one of these people can make a record of your prints.

Crime Lab 1: Recording Fingerprints

It's possible to make a record of your own fingerprints, but it's a lot easier to record someone else's and then let that person record yours. To make a record of a fingerprint, the last digit of the finger is coated with a substance that will show up on paper. Then the finger is placed on paper or sticky tape that reveals the pattern of ridges.

Following are three different methods. The first method uses an ink pad and paper. The second uses graphite from a pencil to coat the fingers; the print is then removed with clear tape. In the third method, the finger is rubbed on carbon paper; the print is then removed with clear sticky tape or by rolling it on a sheet of paper. Choose one method or try all these to see which works best for you.

METHOD 1: Use both hands to grasp the finger that is to be printed. Hold the top of the end of the finger with one hand and the base of the finger with the other hand. Figure 1 shows a print about to be recorded. The "roll" technique is the same as that used to ink the finger. Turn the finger so that the nail above the fingerprint is perpendicular to an ink pad. Then roll the finger's last digit on the pad. The pressure you apply will depend on the amount of ink on the pad. If the pad is new, apply very little pressure. If it's an old pad, apply more

Figure 1   Preparing to record a fingerprint.

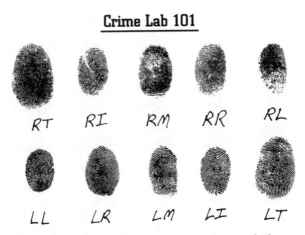

RT RI RM RR RL

LL LR LM LI LT

Figure 2 A set of fingerprints cut out and pasted close together. Notice the pattern left by the scar on the "suspect's" right index finger.

pressure to properly coat the finger. Be sure the finger does not slip as you roll it, or the pattern will be smudged. Use the same motion to record the print on a sheet of paper as shown in Figure 1. The print should clearly reveal the pattern of ridges. You may want to practice the procedure a few times to get the hang of it.

Repeat the process for each finger. The ten patterns can all be recorded on the same sheet of paper and labeled as shown in Figure 2. RT = right thumb, RI = right index finger, RM = right middle finger, RR = right ring finger, RL = right little finger. The symbols for the left hand are the same, except that L is used in place of R.

METHOD 2: Rub the side of the sharpened end of a soft pencil on a sheet of paper. This will transfer some graphite onto the paper. Then have the person whose prints are to be recorded rub the last digit of his or her finger firmly back and forth on the graphite. Next, place a strip of clear, three-quarter-inch-wide plastic tape sticky side down on the graphite-coated finger, as shown in Figure 3. When you

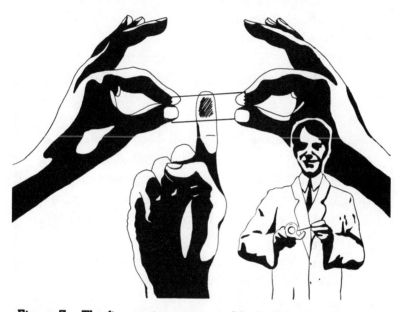

Figure 3 The fingerprint pattern is lifted off the finger with a wide strip of clear sticky tape.

Figure 4 The fingerprint can then be taped onto a sheet of paper.

peel the tape off the finger, the fingerprint pattern will come with it. The tape can then be placed on a sheet of paper as shown in **Figure 4.** How should the tape be placed to match the upturned finger? Can it be turned in such a way as to match the downturned finger?

Repeat the process for each finger. Place the strips on a sheet of paper and label them as described in Method 1.

METHOD 3: Have the person being fingerprinted rub the last digit of his or her finger on a sheet of carbon paper. The carbon will coat the finger. The finger can then be rolled on a sheet of paper as in Method 1, or the print can be removed with tape as in Method 2.

Make records of all the members of your family and some of your friends or classmates. You'll use those records for some of the experiments that follow.

Crime Lab 2: Classifying Fingerprints

Use a magnifying glass to look at the fingerprints. You'll see that they form patterns like those shown in Figure 5. The FBI classifies the patterns as arch, loop, and whorl and then divides each into subcategories to give a total of ten types. You can simply use arch, loop, whorl, and combination. The ridges in an arch pattern come in from one side, rise in the center, and leave on the other side of the print. The lines in a loop pattern enter and leave the

Fingerprints and Other Prints

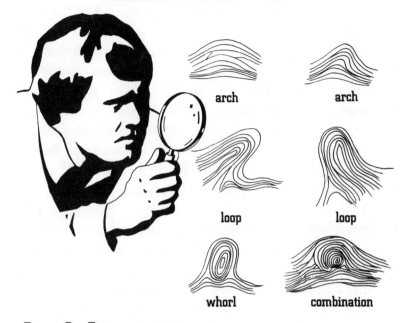

Figure 5 Fingerprint patterns.

same side. A whorl consists of circular lines that don't enter or leave from either side. A combination is a complex arrangement that contains more than one simple pattern.

If you abbreviate arch, loop, whorl, and combinations as A, L, W, and C, you can label a set of prints with formulas. For example, a left thumb print with a whorl pattern would be LTW. A right ring finger print with a combination pattern would be RRC. What would be the formulas for the set of prints seen in Figure 2? What are the formulas for *your* fingerprints? Neglecting right (R) and left (L), are the formulas for both your hands the same? Are they the same for other people?

Fingerprint experts use more complex formulas to classify prints, but the idea is the same. When they are searching for a match between the prints on file and those of a suspect, they look first for a set of formulas that match. This allows them to rule out most of the patterns and concentrate on just those sets of prints in which the formulas are the same.

Crime Lab 3: Using Fingerprint Records

After you've recorded a number of fingerprints, you'll feel confident about the procedure. You might then use the technique you've developed to answer some of the following questions having to do with fingerprint patterns.

○ Which pattern—arch, loop, whorl, or combination—is the most common? Which pattern is least common?

○ Do identical twins have identical fingerprints? If not, are their prints similar? Are their fingerprints mirror images? (That is, if you hold one twin's fingerprints up to a mirror, will you see a match of the other twin's prints?) Do the fingerprints on one twin's right hand match the fingerprints on the other twin's left hand?

○ Why do the police always use the last digit of a person's fingers when making prints?

What do you find if you look at the print made by the entire finger?

○ In addition to the patterns you've seen, what other features that might be used to identify a person can be seen in fingerprints?

○ Can you record your fingerprints in soft clay or plasticene? If you can, why isn't clay used to record fingerprints?

○ Try making fingerprints on a variety of surfaces—glass, Formica, metal, wood, paper, linoleum, cloth, and so on. On which surfaces are fingerprints most easily seen? On which surfaces are they least easily seen?

○ Do the ridges on your fingers that give rise to fingerprints have any use?

○ Look closely at the toes of a dog or cat. Do they have "fingerprints"?

○ When and where were fingerprints first used for purposes of identification?

○ Read Mark Twain's book *The Tragedy of Pudd'nhead Wilson*. When was this book written? Was it the first book to use fingerprint identification as a major part of the plot?

OTHER USEFUL PRINTS

Sometimes a criminal who carefully avoids leaving fingerprints will leave other useful prints such as lip prints, shoe prints, or, if barefoot, footprints or toe prints. These clues can be useful when compared with similar prints taken from suspects.

Crime Lab 101

Owners of expensive horses sometimes record the horses' nose prints. Why do they do this?

Crime Lab 4: Recording Other Prints

Using the same technique you used to make fingerprints, record the toe prints of friends or members of your family. Do a person's toe print patterns match his or her fingerprints? Do you find the same arch, loop, and whorl patterns in toe prints that you found in finger-prints?

Use the same technique to record footprints and palm prints of a number of different peo-ple. Could these prints be used to identify someone present at the scene of a crime?

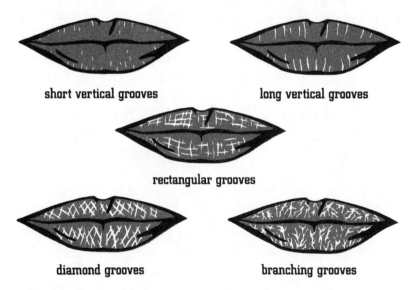

short vertical grooves   long vertical grooves

rectangular grooves

diamond grooves   branching grooves

Figure 6   Common lip-print patterns.

Fingerprints and Other Prints

You've probably seen more lip prints than fingerprints. Women wearing lipstick often leave visible lip prints on glasses from which they have drunk. Lipstick makes it easy to record lip prints. To make such a print, rub a dark lipstick onto both lips. Then rub your lips together to spread the color evenly. Now fold a sheet of white paper, slip the folded paper between your lips, and press your lips firmly against the paper. Be careful not to slide your lips along the paper, or you will smudge the print.

The patterns shown in Figure 6 seem to be quite common, but most people's lips have parts of at least two patterns. Do your lip prints have any of the patterns shown in the drawing?

Record the lip prints of as many people as possible. Do lip prints, like fingerprints, seem to be unique?

The lip prints shown in Figure 7 belong to four women who were at a party. Which woman's lip prints, if any, were left on the drinking glass shown in Figure 8?

LIFTING LATENT FINGERPRINTS

As you've seen, it's easy to make a set of fingerprints. However, finding fingerprints at the scene of a crime and comparing them with the fingerprints of a suspect is more difficult. Sometimes fingerprints made by dirty hands are so clear that they can be easily seen and photographed. But

Figure 7   Lip prints obtained from four different "suspects."

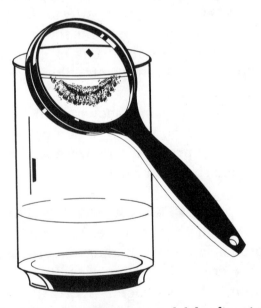

Figure 8   Which, if any, of the four suspects left her lip print on this glass found at the scene of the "crime"?

more often the fingerprints are latent—that is, they cannot be easily seen. Usually someone trained in obtaining fingerprints must use one of several methods to find the fingerprints and then remove or photograph them.

Dusting a surface with a powder sometimes makes fingerprints visible. The powder sticks to the oil along the ridges of the prints. Crime Lab 5 will show you one way to do this.

Crime Lab 5: Lifting Fingerprints and Lip Prints

Lifting fingerprints is not as easy as it appears to be in movies. Even fingerprint experts sometimes find obtaining useful prints difficult. To make your first few attempts easier, rub a drop of cooking oil thoroughly into your fingers. Then make a fingerprint on a small glass dessert plate or a drinking glass. If you turn the plate or glass so that it reflects light from a window or light bulb to your eye, you will probably be able to see the print. In fact, using oblique light (light that strikes the print at a sharp angle) to look for prints on counters, desktops, doorways, telephones, papers, and other places where fingerprints might be expected is a good way to start a fingerprint investigation.

Now that you know where the print is, carefully squeeze a little baby powder or talcum powder onto the surface near the print. If you don't have powder, use cornstarch. Next, using a downy feather or a few wisps of soft cotton as a brush, spread the powder across the print in both directions. This is a very crucial step. *A soft brush is essential!* Something as coarse as a watercolor brush will destroy the print.

At this stage, if the print were clear, a detective would probably photograph it with a special camera. You can do this too if you have a good camera. But you can also lift the print by placing a piece of clear plastic tape on it. When the tape is peeled away, the fingerprint will come with it. Be sure you do not touch the portion of the tape that will cover the print before you apply it.

Compare the lifted print with your own fingerprint record. Can you identify the finger you used to make the print?

Repeat this procedure a few times until you get the hang of it. Then you can try dusting and lifting other people's fingerprints. Finally, you can begin looking for fingerprints on a variety of hard surfaces, dusting and lifting them, and trying to identify the family member or friend who made them.

If your school has ninhydrin powder, try using it to dust latent fingerprints left on paper. Ninhydrin powder is commonly used by crime-lab technicians for making fingerprints on paper visible. Prints dusted with ninhydrin powder will probably take a number of hours to become visible.

Can you find lip prints on drinking glasses or

facial tissues? Can you lift lip prints from drinking glasses or facial tissues? Can you lift lip prints from drinking glasses using the same technique you've used to lift fingerprints? Who left the glass on the kitchen counter?

OTHER METHODS OF LIFTING FINGERPRINTS

In 1932, the baby of Colonel and Mrs. Charles Lindbergh was kidnapped. (Colonel Lindbergh was the first person to make a solo airplane flight across the Atlantic.) A ransom note left in the baby's room was dusted, but no fingerprints were found. Lifting fingerprints from paper or other porous materials is difficult using dusting powder, so Dr. E. M. Hudson, a fingerprint expert, suggested using iodine fuming as a better way to find fingerprints on the ransom note paper. Colonel H. Norman Schwarzkopf, the head of the New Jersey State Police, who was in charge of the case, had not heard of the technique and decided not to pursue Hudson's suggestion.

If he had, Hudson would have placed crystals of iodine in a Pyrex beaker. He would then have heated the beaker in a fume hood because the violet vapors produced when iodine is heated are poisonous. The fans in the fume hood, much like the fan over a kitchen range, would carry the vapors away. Using forceps to hold the note in the violet vapor, Hudson would have found the vapors condensing back to crystals along the pattern of lines left by any fingerprints on the paper.

During the same investigation, Hudson did obtain Schwarzkopf's permission to use another fingerprinting technique, this one using silver nitrate. This method is used to find fingerprints on porous material such as wood. Hudson searched for fingerprints on a ladder found beneath the baby's bedroom window, on the frame of the baby's crib, and on toys in the crib. He did this by spraying a solution of silver nitrate on the materials and then exposing them to sunlight or ultraviolet light. He found plenty of fingerprints on the ladder, but none of them matched those of Bruno Richard Hauptmann, the prime suspect in the case. Hudson suggested that the prints be sent to the FBI to see if they matched any fingerprints on record, but Schwarzkopf declined to do so. He apparently felt that Hauptmann was guilty and that there was no need to search further.

Since 1982, some crime labs have been using cyanoacrylate fuming to develop latent fingerprints. Cyanoacrylate is the chemical found in Superglue. This method is particularly effective in developing latent prints found on aluminum foil, cellophane, rubber bands, Styrofoam, and other plastic products. As the cyanoacrylate vapors condense, they adhere to the body oils along the ridges of the fingerprint, making the pattern visible.

Crime Lab Exercise 1: Developing a Fingerprint with Superglue

If you'd like to try developing latent fingerprints using cyanoacrylate, *ask an adult to help*

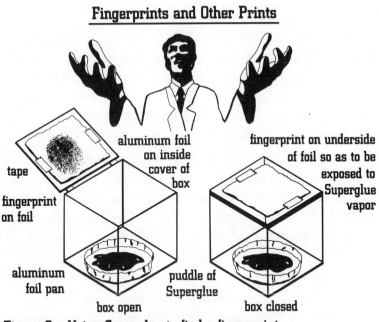

Figure 9   Using Superglue to find a fingerprint.

you. To develop a fingerprint you'll need a small plastic or metal box that will close to make an airtight space. Make a fingerprint on a small piece of aluminum foil. Tape the foil to the *inside* surface of the top of the box as shown in Figure 9. Be sure the fingerprint side of the foil will be exposed to the vapors that will fill the closed box. Make a small pan by folding another piece of aluminum. Place it in the bottom of the box. Squeeze some liquid from a tube of Superglue into the bottom of the small pan you've made. *Be careful not to get the glue on your fingers—it will bond fingers as well as other materials!* Close the box and let the cyanoacrylate vapor from the glue develop the print on the exposed aluminum foil fixed to the inside of the top of the closed box. It will take several hours to develop the fingerprint.

LASERS AND FINGERPRINTS

Some police departments now use lasers to detect latent fingerprints. A portable laser is taken to the scene of a crime by a forensic scientist or a detective trained to use the instrument. If latent fingerprints are made visible in the laser light, they can be photographed or lifted using one of the methods previously discussed.

EYE PRINTS

Other parts of our bodies have unique patterns. Ophthalmologists know that the pattern of blood vessels on the retinas of a person's eyes are unique, just as are fingerprints. At some police departments a person who is arrested and fingerprinted has his or her retinas photographed as well. The suspect looks into a pair of binocularlike lenses and focuses on a target. A scanner photographs the retinal patterns on the backs of the person's eyes. The patterns are stored in the scanner system's computer memory. The computer can compare the retinal patterns it has just "seen" with other patterns stored in its memory to find out if there is a match. The eye scanner and the computer program are made by EyeDentify, Inc.—an appropriately named corporation.

The scanning device is being used by a number

of organizations to which security is important. Some banks use them to identify people seeking access to their safe-deposit boxes. Nuclear weapons plants, missile-launching sites, and other segments of the military use such scanners to ensure that only personnel who have security clearance are admitted to key areas.

Crime Lab Exercise 2: Seeing Your Eye Pattern

The pattern of blood vessels on the back of the eye is called the *Purkinje tree*. You'll sometimes see this pattern during an eye examination. But with a little care, you can see it in any dark room with a good-sized wall surface. The Purkinje tree is usually invisible because its shadow always falls on the same places on the retina. Any fixed image on the retina is quickly bleached by light and disappears. That's why your eye continually makes short, jerky movements when you look at anything. The movements keep the image moving to slightly different places on the retina.

To make the Purkinje tree visible, you need to make its shadow fall on different parts of the retina. You can do this with a strong flashlight in the dark room. Shine the flashlight at your eye from the side or from below the eye as you face the wall. Move the light back and forth through a short distance. After a little while you should be able to see the Purkinje tree. The pattern of blood vessels that you see is the same as the one photographed by the scanner in making eye prints.

FINGERPRINT SCANNERS

Automated fingerprint scanners use a similar procedure with fingerprints. The scanner "looks" at a fingerprint and creates a "map" of the pattern. Its computer then searches a file of fingerprints to find possible matches. The file may be that of a local police station or the vast file of fingerprints at the FBI's Identification Division headquarters.

VOICE PRINTS

When you speak, sound waves travel through the air from your mouth to the ears of those who hear you. If the sound waves reach a microphone, they can generate electrical impulses that can be seen on a TV picture tube. In this way, a print of your voice can be recorded. A voice print, however, is not a fixed pattern. It changes as you speak. Nevertheless, the pattern produced when you speak a given word is quite different from the pattern seen when someone else speaks the same word.

How might voice prints be useful to law-enforcement agencies? Do you think they will ever replace fingerprints as a way of identifying criminals?

DNA PRINTS

Within the nuclei of all the cells of our bodies (except for red blood cells, which have no nuclei) are coiled, threadlike bodies called chromosomes.

These chromosomes are usually paired. Most kinds of human cells have a total of ninety-two chromosomes—forty-six pairs. At the time of conception, when a sperm cell and an egg cell combine, each cell contains only forty-six chromosomes, one member from each pair. Half your chromosomes came from your father's sperm cell; the other half came from your mother's egg cell. Chromosomes are made up of deoxyribonucleic acid, a chemical compound called DNA. DNA provides the "blueprint" that directs the development and operation of our bodies.

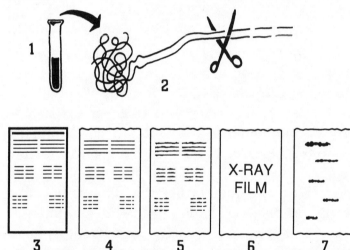

Figure 10   Preparing DNA prints. 1. DNA is extracted from blood cells. 2. DNA is broken into short segments by enzymes. 3. The DNA fragments are separated into bands by electrical means. 4. The DNA bands are transferred to a nylon membrane. 5. Radioactive DNA probes are added to the membrane. 6. X-ray film is placed over the pattern on the membrane. 7. The X-ray film is developed to make a visible DNA print.

Because we all belong to the same species, large strands of DNA are the same in all of us. However, some sections, called junk DNA, differ in all of us except for identical twins. Identical twins come from the same sperm and egg and therefore have identical chromosomes and DNA. Because individuals have unique DNA, DNA prints can be made that are then used to identify crime suspects. The suspects may have worn gloves, but if they left enough body cells, a DNA print as unique as their fingerprints can often be made, as shown in Figure 10 and as follows.

The DNA from cells is first extracted (1) and then "snipped" into shorter sections using enzymes (2). Electrical methods are used to separate the sections by size on a membrane (3 and 4). Next, radioactive probes—DNA molecules that will attach to specific DNA sections that vary from one person to another—are added to the membrane (5). Once the radioactive molecules "find" and attach to specific sections of the DNA, a piece of X-ray film is placed on the membrane (6). The radioactive material produces a change in the X-ray film (just as visible light causes a change in ordinary photographic film), eventually forming a print on the X-ray that reveals the DNA sites where the radioactive probes are located (7).

These DNA prints vary from one individual to another, as shown in Figure 11. DNA extracted from body cells, such as blood cells found at the scene of a crime, can be compared with that ob-

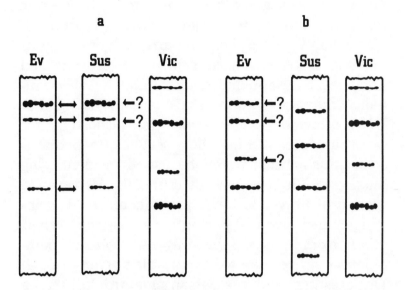

Figure 11   DNA prints from the evidence, the suspect, and the victim. (a) The DNA print from the blood-cell evidence (Ev) matches the DNA print of the suspect (Sus) but not the DNA print from the victim (Vic). (b) The DNA print from the evidence doesn't match the DNA print from the suspect. The suspect is probably innocent.

tained from a suspect to see whether the prints match. Such an analysis is not always possible, however, because the amount of DNA extracted may be insufficient to conduct the test. Some judges are disallowing the use of DNA prints in court cases, ruling, on the basis of testimony and precedents, that the technique is not infallible.

The first use of DNA prints leading to a conviction in the United States was in 1988. The use of DNA prints is a relatively new tool for forensic scientists, and the technique is still being refined. Nevertheless, some police departments are suggesting that DNA prints, as well as fingerprints and photographs, be included in the files of all criminals. Some laboratories are even suggesting that DNA prints be made of all infants shortly after birth and are offering their services to pediatricians. Such prints would be useful in identifying missing children as well as criminals. However, a system of universal DNA prints could lead to infringements upon a person's civil rights. A hair taken from someone handing out political pamphlets could be used to identify the person through DNA testing. With the person's identity known, he or she could be harassed by those with opposing political views. Such universal testing might indeed hinder our right to privacy.

FOUR

Other Clues That Help Solve Crimes

(A) criminal who is careful not to leave finger-prints or other prints may nonetheless leave behind other clues that forensic scientists can use to help police solve the crime. Hair, blood, fibers, broken glass, soil, and other materials may lead police to the guilty party. If bullets were fired during the crime, ballistics experts may be able to learn a great deal by examining slugs, shells, and bullet holes.

Ballistics: Bullets as Evidence

In 1784, Edward Culshaw was shot by someone using a flintlock pistol. In those days, there were no bullets as we know them. Gunpowder and a ball of lead were put into the gun's muzzle and packed with paper wadding. The powder was ignited by a spark made when the gun's hammer struck some flint at the back end of the barrel. When the constable examined Culshaw's wound, he found a piece of newspaper used as wadding to pack the powder in the killer's gun. The prime suspect in the killing was a man named John Toms. When a piece of newspaper found in Toms's pocket was compared with the piece found in the wound, the pieces fit together like two pieces of a jigsaw puzzle. Based on the evidence, Toms was readily convicted. The Toms case was probably the first in America in which ballistics was used to solve a crime. But it was certainly not the last such case.

A bullet fired from a gun moves along a spiral groove in the gun barrel. The spiral groove makes the bullet spin about its axis. To see why bullets in modern guns are made to spin, take a football and throw it the way someone who has never seen a football might throw it, with the ball's long axis perpendicular to the ground. Notice the irregular path it follows. Next throw it the way a good quarterback would; that is, throw a spiral pass. Notice how much faster, farther, and straighter the ball travels this time.

The path followed by a spinning bullet is straight and true. The lead balls shot from old muskets did not spin because the barrels of these guns were not rifled, or spirally grooved. As a result, they were pretty inaccurate at distances greater than a few feet.

A bullet fired from a rifled barrel will have markings—called striations—made on it as it travels down the barrel. The shell that remains in the gun will have scratches made by the firing pin. These markings are unique for each gun. Guns of the same make produce striations that are similar but not identical. By comparing the markings on bullets found at the scene of a crime with those of bullets fired from a suspect's gun, a ballistics expert can often determine if the bullets came from the same gun.

In the 1920s, Philip O. Gravelle invented a microscope through which the images formed by two lenses could be viewed side by side through a single lens. A ballistics expert using this microscope (called a comparison microscope) could compare the images of two bullets and easily tell whether the striations on the two bullets matched.

In 1920, two Italian immigrants, Nicola Sacco and Bartolomeo Vanzetti, were arrested and charged with murdering two men during a payroll robbery in Braintree, Massachusetts. Both suspects were carrying guns as well as literature encouraging people to overthrow the government. At the time, which was shortly after World War I, the country was in dire fear of communists or anyone else who might seek to overthrow the government. Immigrants carrying such literature and guns would probably have found it difficult to obtain a fair trial. In any event, in 1921 Sacco and Vanzetti were convicted and sentenced to death.

In 1927, after reading Felix Frankfurter's book on the Sacco and Vanzetti case, A. Lawrence Lowell, president of Harvard University, asked the governor of Massachusetts to review the case. Frankfurter believed that Sacco and Vanzetti had been convicted as the result of the "social" climate in which they were tried, that the trial had been unfair, and that in fact both men were innocent. In response to Lowell's concern, Governor Alvan T. Fuller appointed Lowell chairman of a committee to investigate the trial.

During its investigation in 1927, the committee asked Colonel Calvin Goddard to review the ballistics evidence. Goddard, using a comparison microscope—which had not been invented at the time of the trial—found that the striations on a bullet found in one of the victims and on bullets fired from Sacco's gun did match. At the trial, the ballistics experts had disagreed on the evidence. After a thorough review, the committee reported that there was no reason for a new trial. Sacco and Vanzetti were executed on August 23, 1927. However, Vanzetti maintained that he was innocent even moments before he was electrocuted. Later, people who had been fellow anarchists said that Sacco was guilty but Vanzetti was innocent. It is possible that Bartolomeo Vanzetti was executed for a crime he did not commit. In any case, Goddard's analysis was confirmed again in 1961 and in 1983 by other ballistics experts.

TOOL MARKS

Just as the barrel of a gun leaves marks on a bullet, so too do tools used to manufacture metal goods. These markings can often lead detectives to the company that manufactured an article found at the scene of a crime. From there, it may be possible to trace the article to the person who purchased it.

A pry bar used by a burglar to break open a door or window may leave characteristic marks. These marks can be checked against those left by a similar tool found in the possession of a suspect. In the case of the woodchipper murder, which you will read about later in this chapter, the marks left on wood chips by a wood-chipping machine were used by forensic scientists to help police prosecute a man suspected of killing his wife.

Crime Lab 6: Testing for Tool Marks

Find a wooden box and put a coin or a candy bar inside. Then nail a top securely on the box. Next, place a variety of tools near the box. You might include a hammer, one or more screwdrivers, some large nails, a chisel, pliers, a wrench, a file, and other tools that *do not have sharp surfaces.* Tell a friend or a family member that he or she can have the contents of the box just by opening it. Explain that any method can be used to open the box using the tools provided. This is to be done when you are not around, and the box and tools are to be left when the job is finished.

When you return to the opened box, examine it carefully for tool marks. Can you determine which tool or tools were used to open the box? Once you have finished your investigation, tell your friend or family member how you think he or she opened the box. Were you right?

Bloody Crimes

Sometimes blood or bloodstains are found at the scene of a crime. By analyzing the blood, laboratory technicians can tell whether it is human. If the blood is not human, the antigens it contains will cause the formation of antibodies in blood serum

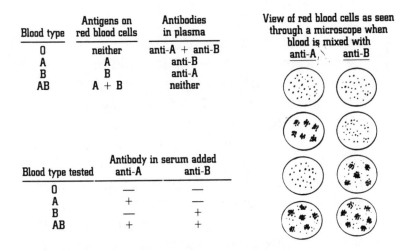

Blood type	Antigens on red blood cells	Antibodies in plasma
O	neither	anti-A + anti-B
A	A	anti-B
B	B	anti-A
AB	A + B	neither

Blood type tested	Antibody in serum added	
	anti-A	anti-B
O	—	—
A	+	—
B	—	+
AB	+	+

Figure 12   Blood types and blood-typing pass tests.
(a) Different blood types, the antigens found on the red blood cells of each type, and the antibodies found in the blood plasma of each type. (b) Testing for blood type: + indicates clumping of red blood cells when the particular antibody is added to the blood being tested. − indicates no clumping. The circled views through the microscope show what is seen when blood cells do or do not clump.

that is human. Those antibodies then react with the antigens. Similar tests can determine the animal from which the blood came. Crime labs routinely test for dog, cat, cow, horse, and chicken blood as well as human.

If the blood is human, the blood type is determined. Human red blood cells may contain one, or both, or neither of two antigens, A and B. Your blood, therefore, can be one of four types—A, B, AB, or O. As you can see from Figure 12a, a person with type-A blood has the A antigen on his or her red blood cells; a person with type-B blood has the B antigen; someone with type-AB blood has both antigens; and a person with type-O blood has neither antigen. Blood plasma may contain antibodies that react with the A or B antigens, causing the blood cells to clump together. Such clumping can prevent the blood from flowing through small blood vessels.

The antibody that reacts with the A antigen is called anti-A; the antibody that reacts with the B antigen is called anti-B. Again, as you can see from Figure 12a, a person with type-AB blood has neither antibody. If she did, her antibodies would react with the antigens on her own red blood cells, causing them to clump.

To find out what blood type a person has, two drops of his or her blood are placed on a glass slide. A drop of blood serum containing the anti-A antibody is added to one drop; a drop of serum containing anti-B is added to the other drop. As you can see from Figure 12*b*, the presence of either anti-A or anti-B will cause type-AB blood to clump. On the other hand, a person with type-O blood carries both antibodies, but neither antigen on his red blood cells. Consequently, his blood cells will not clumb when blood serum with either anti-A or anti-B is added. Someone with type-A blood has the A-antigen and the anti-B antibodies. Her red blood cells will clump when anti-A serum is added but not when anti-B serum is added. Type-B blood, which contains the B-antigen, will clump when anti-B serum is added but not when anti-A serum is added.

Once the blood type of blood found at the scene of a crime has been determined, that information may or may not be useful. Suppose the blood type matches that of the victim and that of the blood found on a knife in the possession of a suspect. Then the knife *could have been* the one used in the crime. However, this is not positive proof. On the other hand, if the blood type or types on the knife do *not* match that of the victim, then we know the knife was *not* used on the victim. Or if it was, it was cleaned before being used on someone else.

The percentages of the people in the United States who have the four blood types are found in the following table. As you can see, type O is the most common, type AB the most rare, and the frequency of each type is related to race. Finding type-AB blood at the scene of a crime can be very useful in reducing the list of suspects, whereas type-O blood would likely only eliminate half of the suspects.

Blood Type	White (%)	Black (%)
O	45	49
A	40	27
B	11	20
AB	4	4

Blood types A, B, AB, and O are not the only ones used by crime labs. Human blood contains other antigens for which tests have been developed. Crime labs routinely test for Rh (+ or −), M and N, and Le antigens as well as a number of blood enzymes. By using all of these tests, investigators may clear a high percentage of suspects of any wrongdoing. But, unlike fingerprints, blood-type evidence cannot provide proof of guilt. It can only reduce the number of individuals who might be guilty of a crime.

GLASSY CLUES

Broken glass is often found at the scene of a crime. Burglars, robbers, and kidnappers often break windows in order to enter locked buildings. Glass objects may be broken during a fight, robbery, or murder. Tiny particles of the glass may become lodged in a criminal's clothing or shoes. If such fragments are found on a suspect, forensic scientists test the glass to see if it could have come from the scene of the crime.

In testing glass, forensic scientists measure its density and color. The density of a substance is its weight per volume, that is, how much a certain volume of the material weighs. For example, 100 milliliters of water weighs 100 grams, so each milliliter of water weights 1 gram. The density of water, therefore, is 1 gram per milliliter.

Forensic scientists usually have only very small pieces of glass to work with; consequently, they use very accurate and sensitive instruments. If the density of the glass particles found on a suspect matches the density of the glass found at the scene of a crime, it's possible the suspect was there. If the samples don't match, it's certain the glass on the suspect did not come from the crime scene.

Crime Lab Exercise 3: Measuring the Density of Glass and Plastic

The instruments used to measure the density of tiny pieces of glass are very expensive. However, you can make similar measurements on a much larger scale with less expensive instruments.

For a piece of glass, you can use a small jam or jelly jar. First, weigh the empty jar—without the lid—on a balance. How many grams (or ounces) does your sample of glass weigh?

Now find the volume of the glass you weighed. If you used a small jar, fill a measuring cup with water to a level high enough to cover the jar when you submerge it. What is the volume in milliliters or ounces of the water in the measuring cup? Gently place the jar in the measuring cup. Be sure it is completely submerged. Look at the water level in the measuring cup now. What is the *total* volume? What is the volume of the glass jar?

Now that you know the volume and weight of your sample of glass, you can find its density. Simply divide its weight in grams or ounces by its volume in milliliters or ounces. For example, in one experiment an amateur sleuth found that a small jelly jar weighed 85 grams (3 ounces) and had a volume of 30 milliliters (1 fluid ounce). From these measurements, he found how much 1 milliliter weighed by dividing 85 grams by 30 milliliters. In other words, he found the density to be

$$\frac{85 \text{ grams}}{30 \text{ milliliters}}$$

$$= 2.8 \text{ grams/milliliter or } \frac{3 \text{ ounces}}{1 \text{ fluid ounce}}$$

$$= 3 \text{ ounces/fluid ounce}.$$

What is the density of your glass sample?

Now repeat the experiment with a small plastic container or another sample of glass. How do the densities of the two containers compare?

Figure 13 Light that enters a glass block is bent. It is bent again but in the opposite way when it emerges from the glass into the air. As you can see, some light is also reflected at each surface.

How might the color or shape of or scratches and designs on glass articles be used by a forensic scientist? Experiment with these properties and try to establish a set of reliable methods by which you can identify clues from glass articles. *Be careful not to cut yourself.*

THE REFRACTIVITY OF GLASS

Forensic scientists might also try to match glass samples by testing the refractivity of the glass. Refractivity is a measure of the amount that light is bent by the glass. The bending of light when it passes from one transparent substance, such as air, to another, such as water, is called refraction. Some substances refract (bend) light a lot; other substances, such as air, bend light hardly at all. Glass refracts light more than air or water, but not nearly as much as diamond. Some kinds of glass bend light more than other kinds. These differences in refractivity are what enable forensic scientists to match even small samples of glass.

Figure 13 shows how a beam of light bends when it enters and leaves glass. As you can see from the photograph, some of the light that strikes the upper surface of the glass block is reflected. Similarly, some of the light that has passed through the glass is reflected back to the upper surface while some is bent as it emerges from the lower surface. The refractivity of a transparent substance such as glass is a measurement of how much it bends light.

Crime Lab Exercise 4: Bending Light with Water

You can do a very simple experiment to show that light bends when passing from water to air. Just place a pencil or a stick in a glass of water and look at it from the side. Notice how the stick appears to be broken at the point where it enters the water. The light reflected from the pencil that comes through the water is bent when it enters the air. That's why the submerged part of the pencil seems dislocated from the upper part.

For more direct evidence that light bends when it passes from one transparent material to another, use the materials shown in Figure

14. The mask is made from a rectangle cut from black construction paper. The narrow slit was cut in the center of the mask using a pair of scissors. It is placed close to the clear flat-sided container of water and several meters from a bright light bulb. The rest of the room should be dark so that you can see the light beam clearly. What happens to the light beam when it enters the water? What happens to the light beam when it comes out of the water on the other side of the box?

TESTING REFRACTIVITY IN A CRIME LAB

When crime-lab technicians try to match glass samples, they check to see if the samples refract light in the same way. Of course, the glass tested in

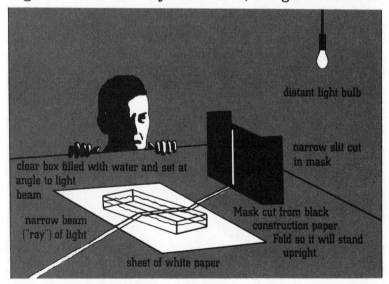

Figure 14   Bending light with water.

a crime lab usually consists of small pieces. Generally, the glass samples used as evidence are too small to bend a narrow beam of light. But suppose you had a transparent liquid that refracted light in exactly the same way as a certain kind of glass. If you placed the glass in the liquid, the glass would disappear! As far as light is concerned, the glass and the liquid are the same substances because they both refract light the same way. Forensic scientists use this property to help determine the refractivity of glass samples found at the scene of a crime.

In a crime lab, the glass samples from the scene of the crime and from the suspect are suspended in a clear silicone oil. The oil is then warmed or cooled because the refractive properties of the oil change with temperature. When one of the glass samples disappears, the investigator knows that it has the same refractive property as the silicone at that temperature. If both glass samples disappear at the same temperature, the observer knows that the samples refract light in the same way. If their densities also match, the two samples may well have come from the same source. On the other hand, if either the density or the refractive properties of the glass don't match, the glass found on the suspect did not come from the scene of the crime.

Crime Lab Exercise 5: Matching Refractivities

Find some *transparent* plastic tape. Be sure it is really transparent. Some plastic tape is a bit foggy. The clear tape refracts light in almost exactly the same way as clear or light-colored cooking oil, which you can buy in any super-market or grocery store. Pour some of the clear cooking oil into a clear glass or beaker. Now dip one end of a strip of transparent plastic tape into the oil. What happens to the visibil-ity of the end of the tape submerged in the oil?

If your school has some glass stirring rods, ask if you may borrow one. You can use it in place of the transparent tape. Put the stirring rod in a beaker that contains the clear cooking oil. It will bend (refract) light the same (or nearly the same) amount as the glass rod. You'll see the bottom of the stirring rod disappear just as it does in the photograph in Figure 15. If the glass and liquid don't have *exactly* the same refractive properties, you'll be able to see the submerged glass if you look closely.

A Body Is Found

Examining a corpse is not a pleasant experience. Examining a body dead for some time is even worse; there may be maggots on and in the body. Although coroners do not like to examine a body that is decaying or infested with insects, the pres-ence of such organisms helps them to determine how long the victim has been dead. The blowflies that lay eggs on a dead body go through a life cycle that consists of the egg, three larval stages, a pupa,

Figure 15 The refractivity of the glass and the refractivity of the cooking oil are the same. As a result, light can't "tell" them apart. The part of the glass rod submerged in cooking oil disappears.

and finally the adult fly. The entire cycle takes about ten days in warm weather and twice as long in cool weather.

In one case, a coroner determined from the larvae on a body that the victim had been dead five days. Of three suspects, only one had been in the vicinity at that time. When presented with the evidence, he confessed to the murder.

In bodies found shortly after death, the jaw and limbs may be stiff. This stiffness, called rigor mortis, begins in the jaw about eight to twelve hours after death and spreads to the limbs. After about a day, rigor mortis disappears as tissues begin to soften with decay.

The victim's body temperature can also help in

determining the time of death. It falls toward the temperature of the surroundings at a rate that depends on the amount of body fat, on the clothing worn, and on weather conditions such as air temperature, wind, and precipitation (rain or snow).

A coroner examining a dead body looks closely for wounds, abrasions, and rope marks in order to determine the cause of death. Photographs are taken, as are fingerprints. The coroner will note such characteristics as eye and hair color, height, weight, scars, tattoos, number of teeth and type of dental work, and any indications of occupation. (For example, the fingertips of a coal miner might have blue scars from tiny particles of coal dust that have penetrated the skin. The hair and clothing of a carpenter might contain small bits of sawdust.) The stomach and bladder contents are taken for analysis, and vital organs are removed. If poison is suspected, a toxicologist will analyze the blood, urine, and stomach contents. Poisons such as lead will show up in the bone tissue, and arsenic will show up in the hair.

In the case of drowning, a fine, frothy foam will be found through the respiratory tract, the lungs will be soggy, and the stomach will contain water. Some of the water that enters the lungs when a drowning victim gasps for air will seep into the left side of the heart, diluting the blood there. If the victim was dead before entering the water, the heart blood will be undiluted.

Crime Lab 7: Using Temperature to Determine Elapsed Time

As you've read, the temperature of a body can sometimes be used to determine the time of death. Temperature might also be used to find out how much time has passed since someone left an undrunk cup of coffee.

Have someone agree to pour and leave a cup of coffee in your kitchen. Assume the person left soon after the coffee was poured. Begin your investigation by recording the time and the temperature of the coffee. Then pour a fresh cup of coffee of the same volume into a similar cup. Measure the temperature of the fresh coffee at one-minute intervals. Record your temperature and time information in two columns side by side. How long did it take for the temperature of the second cup of coffee to reach the temperature of the first cup of coffee? About how long had the coffee you discovered been sitting in your kitchen? At about what time did the person who had poured the coffee leave it?

A SKELETON IS FOUND

In some cases, a death may have occurred so long ago that only the skeleton remains. This makes the task of identifying the victim much more difficult. However, forensic anthropologists, people who study the bone structure of ancient and modern humans, can learn a great deal from bones. For example, the shape and size of hipbones and sacrum, the skull, and the leg bones are different in men and women. It may also be possible to identify racial features such as the high, narrow nose bones of a Caucasian. The sinuses are as unique as fingerprints. In fact, following the assassination of President John F. Kennedy in 1963, Clyde Snow, a well-known forensic anthropologist, used X-rays of Kennedy's forehead to prove that the man murdered in Dallas really was Kennedy. Some had claimed the event was part of a conspiracy and the man murdered was not the president!

Babies, as you've probably heard, have soft spots in their heads because the bones that make up the skull have not fused. In fact, these bones don't completely fuse until about the age of twenty-five. By examining the skull, anthropologists can approximate the age if the victim was young.

The length of leg bones can be used to estimate the height of the victim. In fact, there is a formula for doing this. The size of ridges on the bones where muscles attach indicate the strength and size of the victim's musculature. Larger ridges on the left arm would suggest that the person was left-handed. A broken hyoid bone, which lies near the larynx (Adam's apple), might indicate the victim was strangled. Holes in the ribs or skull may mark the penetration of a bullet.

In 1985, Clyde Snow and other investigators traveled to Brazil to examine an exhumed skeleton said to be that of Josef Mengele, the Nazi "Angel of Death." Mengele had been wanted since World War II for carrying out atrocities on people confined to concentration camps during the war. From the skeletal remains removed from a grave in São Paulo, Snow was able to show that the dead man's height, stature, and age were consistent with records describing Mengele. Later, when Mengele's dental records were discovered, the match with the teeth of the skeleton made his identity positive.

However, forensic anthropologists were quite certain the skeleton was that of Mengele long before the confirming proof from dental records was available. Richard Helmer, a German anthropologist, had superimposed images of the reconstructed skull found in São Paulo on photographs of Mengele. The match convinced the investigators that they had found the remains of Mengele.

Crime Lab 8: Investigating Animal "Crimes"

If you live near woods, parks, or fields that you can walk through, you will occasionally see the remains of a dead animal. Here is an opportunity to use your crime-detecting skills. *Don't touch the remains,* but use a stick to turn the animal so that you can see it more clearly. What kind of animal was it? Do you think the animal died recently or a long time ago? Was it young or old? Are there feathers? Fur? Can you find tracks or other clues that help you determine whether the animal was killed or just died?

If only a skeleton remains, can you determine what animal it was? Did it have antlers? If you can find a book with pictures of animal skeletons, you can compare the skeleton you found with those of known animals in the book. You might take a photograph of the skeleton you found to make the comparison easier.

FORENSIC SCULPTORS

Betty Pat Gatliff, a medical artist who has worked with Clyde Snow, can reconstruct a three-dimensional sculpture of a face from a skull. She uses known values of the thickness of the flesh over specific parts of the skull to produce her work. Recently developed computer software can do the same job. In fact, the software can create an age-adjusted picture of the face. Such software allows a computer to produce a picture that shows what a child who has been missing for several years might look like today.

In early 1989, the TV program "America's Most Wanted" used a sculpture to show an age-adjusted bust of a man who had been missing since 1971. The bust was made by Frank Bender, who had done a number of forensic reconstructions before. He used old photographs of the missing man to guide him while taking into account the effects on the man's face of eighteen years of aging. The man, John List, a former resident of Westfield, New Jersey, had shot his wife, mother, and three children before he disappeared.

After the program, police received 300 calls from

viewers who claimed to know where John List could be found. In following up one lead, FBI agents called at the home of Mr. and Mrs. Robert Clark in Richmond, Virginia. Mrs. Clark, who was alone at home, was stunned by the obvious resemblance of her husband to the old pictures of John List and to the photograph of the reconstructed bust done by Bender.

When the agents talked to Mr. Clark, who was working as an accountant in Richmond, he denied ever having been anyone but Robert Clark. However, a scar behind his ear indicated that he had undergone a type of surgery that police knew had been performed on List. But even more incriminating was the evidence that led to his arrest: His fingerprints matched those of John List.

Crime Lab 9: Making a Drawing to Identify a "Criminal"

When a witness has seen the person who committed a crime, police will often ask the witness to describe the criminal to a police artist. The artist then draws the criminal's face while the witness watches and suggests changes to make the face resemble the criminal's as much as possible. You may have seen such drawings in a newspaper. People who see the drawing in a newspaper or a wanted-person poster may recognize the wanted person and report the suspect to the police.

If you can draw well, you can be the artist in

this "investigation." If not, ask a friend with artistic talents to help you. Ask someone to describe one of his or her relatives or friends whom you have never seen. From the description, you or your friend can begin to draw a face that matches the description. As the drawing progresses, the friend who is playing the role of the witness should offer suggestions to make the drawing resemble the person as closely as possible.

When the drawing is complete, show the "criminal" face to people who know the person whose face has been drawn. Can they identify the "guilty" party?

If you or a friend can sculpt, you might prepare a three-dimensional likeness of the "criminal" rather than a drawing.

BITE MARKS AND FORENSIC DENTISTRY

Sometimes criminals in a fit of emotion bite their victims, leaving incriminating bite marks. In other cases, old bite marks can be made visible by shining ultraviolet light on a victim's skin. Melanocytes—skin cells that produce the dark pigment responsible for tanning—form around the margins of wounds. These pigmented cells absorb ultraviolet light. If old bite wounds are illuminated by ultraviolet light, the bite marks appear and may be photographed with a scale, such as a ruler, beside them. A forensic dentist can then compare these bite marks with those of a suspect to see if they match.

Crime Lab 10: Making and Examining Bite Prints

To see what your bite print looks like, take a piece of paper and fold it as shown in Figure 16a. Then fold a piece of carbon paper, carbon side out (Figure 16b), and place it inside the folded sheet of paper (Figure 16c). Now bite down on the paper (Figure 16d). When you unfold the paper, you can see your bite pattern.

How does your bite pattern compare with the bite pattern of other members of your

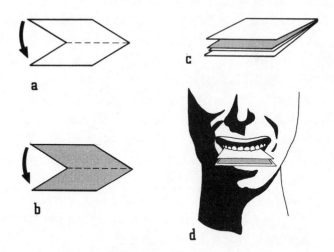

Figure 16   Making a bite print. (a) Fold a small sheet of white paper. (b) Fold a small sheet of carbon paper, carbon side out. (c) Place the carbon paper inside the white paper. (d) Place the folded paper between your teeth and bite down.

family? With the bite patterns of your friends and classmates? Do bite patterns seem to be unique? Make a file of the bite patterns you have collected.

Look closely at an apple, a candy, a sandwich, or some other partially eaten food that has bite marks in it. Compare the bite marks you see with the bite prints in your file. Can you tell who partially ate the food?

Forensic Dentistry and the Woodchipper Murder

In a case known as the Woodchipper Murder, forensic dentistry played a very important role. Richard Crafts had been accused of killing his wife, Helle; cutting her body into parts, which he placed in plastic bags; and then shredding the parts with a woodchipper he had rented. Crafts claimed that his wife, a flight attendant, had gone to visit her mother while on a flight to Europe. This was a false lead. The police talked to her mother, who knew nothing of such a visit. Crafts told police that he had rented the woodchipper to dispose of some limbs that had fallen during a snowstorm. However, a witness claimed to have seen Crafts using the woodchipper near a river not far from his home at 4:00 A.M. during a snowstorm.

Police sifted through the debris found at the site where the witness claimed Crafts had been working. They found pieces of bone, fingernail, toenail, teeth, dental crowns, fingers, hairs, and plastic.

They also found in the nearby river a chainsaw owned by Crafts. A forester testified that the marks on wood chips found near the river matched those found on chips in a woodlot near Crafts's home and in the back of his truck.

Dr. C. P. Karazulas, a forensic dentist, testified that after taking hundreds of X-rays at many angles he had identified one tooth and one gold crown as having come from Helle Crafts. His analysis was confirmed by a second forensic dentist, Dr. Lowell Levine.

HAIR AND FIBERS

Hairs found at the same riverbank location as Helle Crafts's tooth and crown were found to match the hairs taken from her hairbrush. Although the shape of hair shafts is not unique, hers happened to show "shouldering," a protrusion from the hair shaft, which is very rare.

In other cases, fibers from clothing have often been matched with fibers from a suspect. It was the yellow-green nylon fibers on the victims of an Atlanta, Georgia, serial killer that led to the killer's arrest.

Wayne Williams became a prime suspect in the case when police, after hearing a splash in the river beneath a bridge, saw Williams's car pull away. Two days later, the twelfth young victim of a serial killer was discovered downriver. Fibers found in Williams's car matched those found on the body. Fibers found on other victims matched fibers in

Williams's bedroom carpet. Police tracked down the carpet manufacturer. From the limited production of this type of carpeting, they showed that only 82 carpets (1 in very 7,792 carpets) of this type could be expected to be found in all of Georgia. Another victim had been found with fibers that matched those in the carpet of Williams's car. The likelihood of another car with the same carpeting was 1 in 3,828. Thus, the probability of victims carrying fibers from both Williams's bedroom and car was $1/7,792 \times 1/3,828$ or $1/29,827,776$. The odds were clearly against Williams, and he was convicted.

Crime Lab 11: Examining Hair and Fibers

Use a microscope to look at fibers pulled from various types of cloth and carpeting. Can you distinguish between wool and cotton fibers? Can you distinguish cotton from silk? Nylon from acetate?

Using a microscope or a good hand lens, examine several hairs pulled from your head. Do they look the same? Compare them with hair samples provided by friends and members of your family. Can you detect differences? How do they compare with hairs shed by a cat or a dog? Make a file of the hairs you collect.

Look for hairs on furniture, carpets, or clothing. Examine them closely with a hand lens or microscope. Did they come from a human or an animal? Find some that are human in origin.

Compare them with hairs in your file. Can you determine from whose head the hair came?

CLUES ARE NOT LIMITED TO FINGERPRINTS

As you have seen, forensic scientists can make use of a great variety of evidence. Criminals who are careful not to leave fingerprints often leave a variety of other evidence such as bullets, blood, hairs, fibers, glass, and bite marks. Such evidence may be more difficult to trace and match with a suspect than a nice clear set of fingerprints, but it is often enough to convict a criminal who thought he or she had left no clues.

FIVE

DOCUMENTS AND CRIME

(K) idnappers often leave ransom notes. Suicide victims frequently leave notes, and forgery, fraud, counterfeiting, and embezzlement are crimes that involve false documents. Crime labs are constantly being called upon to test documents in various ways.

HANDWRITING AS EVIDENCE

The conviction of Bruno Richard Hauptmann, who was arrested for the kidnapping of the Lindbergh baby, was based in part on the testimony of handwriting experts. They compared the writing on the ransom note with handwriting samples that the police obtained from Hauptmann after his arrest. Part of the testimony involved the similarity between the misspelled words on the ransom note with the same misspelled words written by Hauptmann under police supervision. What was not made clear was that Hauptmann had been told exactly what words to write and how to spell (or misspell) them by the police. A review of letters written by

Hauptmann before his arrest shows that he was a reasonably good speller, considering the fact that he was an immigrant who had lived in America for only a few years.

The next crime lab will give you a chance to see how well you fare at handwriting analysis.

Crime Lab 12: Identifying Handwriting

Ask members of your family and some friends to provide samples of their handwriting. For example, each of them might write their name and address on one side of a file card and a short note on the other side. Then ask them to select one or two persons from among them to write you a mystery note. Your task is to use the note and the handwriting samples to determine who wrote the note.

What factors do you look for as you try to determine who wrote the mystery message? Are certain letters as es, as, and os made in a distinctive fashion? Are there open loops in the ts? In the ds? The ks? Does the writing slant one way or the other? Are certain words misspelled? You might want to go back and dictate certain passages to prime suspects to see how their writing or spelling compares with certain key words in the message. It would be wise not to ask for single words but to "hide" the key words within a longer passage to keep them off guard.

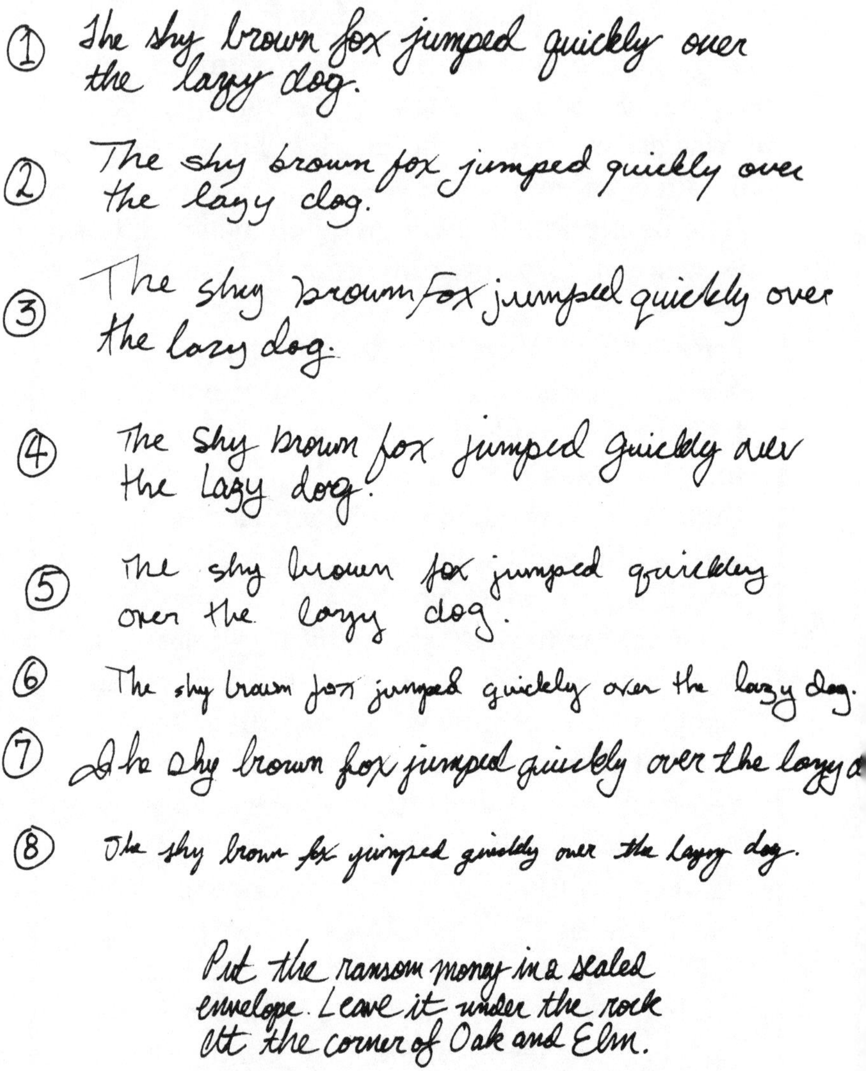

① The shy brown fox jumped quickly over the lazy dog.

② The shy brown fox jumped quickly over the lazy dog.

③ The shy brown fox jumped quickly over the lazy dog.

④ The shy brown fox jumped quickly over the lazy dog.

⑤ The shy brown fox jumped quickly over the lazy dog.

⑥ The shy brown fox jumped quickly over the lazy dog.

⑦ The shy brown fox jumped quickly over the lazy d

⑧ The shy brown fox jumped quickly over the lazy dog.

Put the ransom money in a sealed envelope. Leave it under the rock at the corner of Oak and Elm.

Figure 17   Eight handwriting samples are shown with the "ransom" note at the bottom. Can you identify which handwriting sample matches the writing in the ransom note? Can you explain why the "suspects" were asked to write the particular sentence found in the samples?

Can you identify the person who wrote the note?

By the middle of the school year your teacher can probably identify your handwriting and that of all your classmates as well. If your teacher is willing, ask him or her to identify a mystery note written by a member of the class. Could your teacher identify the writer of the note? Ask your teacher what clues he or she used in identifying the handwriting.

Can you identify which "suspect" wrote the ransom note shown at the bottom of Figure 17?

WATERMARKS IN DETECTIVE WORK

If you hold a sheet of writing paper at an angle to a light, you may be able to see the impression of the manufacturer's name or emblem on the blank sheet. This is called a watermark. It was made by pressing the paper while it was still wet during its manufacture. The compressed wood fibers in the paper reflect light better than the other fibers in the paper. As a result, we can see the words or emblems when light reflects off them.

After a railroad strike led by Eugene Debs's American Railway Union in 1894, railroad managers used a watermark to blacklist any workers who had been active in the strike. At first, the managers simply refused to write letters for former workers seeking employment after the strike had been broken. When the courts awarded damages to a worker who sued the company because the managers would not give him a letter acknowledging his service, the managers resorted to more subtle methods.

On each service letter was a watermark visible only in strong light. The watermark depicted a crane (bird). If the employee had not been active in the strike, the crane stood with its head erect. But if the man seeking employment had been actively involved in the strike, the crane's head hung down as if it had a broken neck. A manager examining the papers of a man looking for work would simply look for the watermark. If the crane's neck were down, the man was denied a job.

Have you ever written a note on hard surface with another sheet of paper beneath the paper you're writing on? If you have, you may have noticed that by holding the paper at an angle to the light you can read the words you wrote from the impressions made on the blank sheet of paper. You have made your own "watermarks."

Crime Lab 13: Reading "Blank" Sheets of Paper

Search your desktop for sheets of paper that were beneath papers you've written on. Look at them in bright light or hold them at an angle to the light. How many messages can you find on these blank sheets of paper?

Obtain permission from friends or family members to look at the papers on their desktops. How many of their messages can you decipher?

Ask a parent to use a ballpoint pen to write his or her shopping list on a pad. Then offer to tell your parent what's on the shopping list using the blank sheet of paper that was beneath the shopping list.

Suppose the blank paper is damp, as it might be in humid weather. Will the watermarks left on damp or wet paper be easier to read than those made on dry paper? Do you think a watermark message on dry paper will be more visible if you wet the paper? Try it! What do you find? Would a detective try wetting blank papers at the scene of a crime to look for watermark messages?

Crime Lab 14: Identifying Types of Paper

The watermark found on paper at the scene of a crime might match the watermark on paper in the possession of a suspect. Such a match would provide additional evidence for a case. Also useful might be identifying the type of paper on which a note was written. For example, a note written on computer paper might suggest the innocence of a suspect who did not own or have access to a computer.

Collect several sheets of a number of different types of paper—adding-machine, blotter, bond, computer, copier, duplicator, facsimile (fax), note, typewriter, wrapping, and so on. Have a friend cut a square from one sheet of any of the samples of paper you have collected and write a note on it. He or she should leave the note where you can find it. Your job as a crime detector is to identify the type of paper on which the note was written. If your friend left the cut sheet where you could find it, your task would be easy. Therefore, be sure to tell your friend to remove the sheet of paper after writing the note.

Try to match the paper on which the note is written with the samples that you have collected. You can quickly compare the color, thickness, and feel of the paper and the samples. Hold the paper and samples in front of a bright source of light, such as a window on a sunny day. Compare the amount of light that comes through the samples with the amount that comes through the paper on which the note is written. Compare the amount of light reflected by the note and each sample when they are held together at a sharp angle to the light.

Tear a corner of the note and look with a good magnifying glass or a microscope at the wood fibers in the paper. Compare the fibers in the paper on which the note is written with those in the samples you've collected. Do some match better than others?

Based on all your comparisons, which paper do you think your friend used to write the note? Check with your friend to see if you are right.

Crime Lab 15: Writing with Invisible Ink

Some blank sheets of paper may contain messages even though the paper has no watermark. A message with invisible ink, for example, must first be developed before it can be read. To see how such a message might be written and then developed, you'll need paper, lemon juice, and a flat toothpick. The lemon juice is your invisible ink. Dip the broad end of the toothpick in the lemon juice frequently as you write an invisible message on the paper.

After the lemon juice has dried, you can develop the writing. To do this, *ask an adult to help you heat the paper above a candle flame or over the heating element of a kitchen range*. Use forceps to hold the card, and be careful not to set it on fire. (To be on the safe side, place a pan of water on the stove. Should the paper catch fire, drop it into the water.) Hold the paper far enough above the flame or heater so that it becomes warm but not hot. You'll see your message slowly reveal itself before your eyes.

Lemon juice is not the only invisible ink. If your school has cobalt chloride, ask your teacher to help you make a solution of the crystals. Dissolve as many of the cobalt chloride crystals as possible in a small amount (about 10 milliliters) of water. Then, with a toothpick, write another invisible message using cobalt chloride "ink."

To make the message visible, heat the card as you did before *under adult supervision*. This time the invisible ink will turn blue as the chemically held water in the pink cobalt chloride crystals is driven away by heat.

Suppose you wanted to write a secret message in invisible ink and there was no lemon juice around. You might try using something you always have with you—saliva. Can something as simple as saliva be used as an invisible ink? To find out, use another toothpick to write a message. This time wet the toothpick with saliva and write the message on a blank sheet of paper. When the "ink" has dried, heat the card as you did before *under adult supervision*. Can saliva be used as invisible ink?

Crime Lab 16: Identifying the Pen Used to Write a Ransom Note

A suspect in a kidnapping case has been placed in custody. In her jacket was found a felt-tip pen with black ink, the same color ink used to write the ransom note. To see if the ink in the suspect's pen matches the ink on the ransom note, a chromatography test is conducted. The word *chromatography* comes from *chromo,* meaning "color," and *graphy*—"to write" or "arrange graphically." As you will see, chromatography separates colored substances along what might be considered the axis of a graph.

To see what a chromatography test is, first collect several different felt-tip and ballpoint pens that all have black ink. Then cut some strips about one inch wide and six inches long from coffee filters or white blotting paper. About an inch from one end of a strip, draw a narrow line with one of the pens. On separate strips of coffee filter or blotter paper, draw similar lines with each of the black pens you have collected. In Figure 18a, you see the strips with the lines marked on them suspended by strips of tape from a long strip or rod. The tips of the lower ends of the strips, below where the black lines have been drawn,

a   tape   stick   paper strips

water in container

Ink lines drawn with different pens.

stack of books

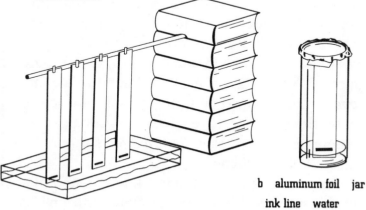

b   aluminum foil   jar

ink line   water

Figure 18   Using chromatography to identify inks.

should just touch the surface of the water in a wide container. Notice how water moves up each of the strips. What happens when the water reaches the ink?

Leave the strips for an hour or so. If the air is very dry, the water may not carry the dyes in the ink far enough to separate them. If that is the case, support the strips in a tall bottle or jar as shown in Figure 18b. By covering the top with aluminum foil, you'll reduce the evaporation rate. Water will then travel farther up the paper strip.

Are all the inks the same? How do you know?

If you use an ink that will not dissolve in water, the ink will not move up the paper strip. Of course, knowing that an ink is *not* soluble in water is one way to help identify an unknown pen. It may be possible to separate the ink into different pigments if another liquid is used in place of water. For example, if you find an ink that won't dissolve in water, try using rubbing alcohol in place of water. Because alcohol evaporates faster than water, you'll want to use a bottle or a jar to enclose the paper strip. Remember, *alcohol is flammable. Do not use alcohol near a flame!*

Ask a friend to make a mark at one end of a coffee filter or blotter paper strip with one of several pens after you leave the room. When you return, determine which pen your friend used by making a chromatogram of each pen's ink as well as the strip that contains the unknown ink. Which pen was used? How could you test the ink in a suspect's pen to see if it matches the ink found on a ransom note?

Have your friend write a note with one of several pens. What can you do to identify which pen might have been used to write the note?

You might like to run chromatography tests on a variety of different-colored pens. For example, from what you have learned in art class, what pigments, other than green, might you expect to find in green ink? Are these pigments the same in all green inks? How about the ink in red pens? What colored pigments might it contain? In blue pens? Yellow? Orange? Brown?

TYPEWRITERS AS EVIDENCE

In many mystery novels or TV shows, the criminal is caught because he or she used a typewriter that made a unique *g, h i,* or some other character. In 1950, in a very controversial case, Alger Hiss was convicted of perjury (giving false testimony while under oath) largely because of evidence involving the rather unusual print produced by a typewriter. The prosecution claimed that Hiss had used the typewriter in copying certain State Department documents that were then forwarded to the Soviet Union.

Crime Lab 101

In the next Crime Lab you'll look for typewriter flaws or characteristic print to see if you can distinguish among particular typewriters.

Crime Lab 17: Comparing Type

Try to gather together a number of letters or sheets of information prepared on different typewriters. Can you distinguish printing from different typewriters? Do the letters have breaks or other distinctive marks? Do you think you could use the samples to identify the typewriters used to make them?

Ask a friend to write you a note using any one of the typewriters from which you have sample print. Your friend is to do this in your absence so that you have no idea which typewriter was used. Using your samples of typewriter print, can you identify the typewriter used to write the note?

Look at the samples of typewriter print in Figure 19. Can you identify the typewriter used to print the "ransom note" at the bottom?

Today fewer letters are written on typewriters. Word processors or computers and printers have made writing and rewriting so much easier that typewriters are rapidly becoming obsolete. Collect samples of letters or printed material from a number of different word processors or printers used to print letters from various computer software programs. Again, ask a friend to obtain printed matter from one

The shy brown fox jumped quickly over the lazy dog.
THE SHY BROWN FOX JUMPED QUICKLY OVER THE LAZY DOG.

The shy brown fox jumped quickly over the lazy dog.
THE SHY BROWN FOX JUMPED QUICKLY OVER THE LAZY DOG.

The shy, brown fox junped quickly over the lazy dog.
THE SHY, BROWN FOX JUMPED QUICKLY OVER THE LAZY DOG.

The shy brown fox jumped quickly over the lazy dog.
THE SHY BROWN FOX JUMPED QUICKLY OVER THE LAZY DOG.

The shy, brown fox jumped quickly over the lazy dog
THE SHY, BROWN FOX JUMPED QUICKLY OVER THE LAZY DOG.

The shy brown fox jumped quickly over the lazy dog.
THE SHY BROWN FOX JUMPED QUICKLY OVER THE LAZY DOG

The shy brown fox jumped quickly over the lazy dog.
THE SHY BROWN FOX JUMPED QUICKLY OVER THE LAZY DOG.

Put the ransom money
in a sealed envelope.
Leave it under the big
rock at thecorner of
Oak and Elm.

Figure 19 Seven samples of print taken from seven different typewriters as well as a "ransom" note at the bottom. Which of the seven typewriters sampled could have been used to type the ransom note? How did you identify the "guilty" typewriter?

79

of the machines for which you have a print sample. Can you determine which machine or software program it came from? Can you distinguish the print from two word processors that are the same model? From two computers and printers that are identical models?

COUNTERFEITING

The Secret Service was originally established to track down and arrest people who were making counterfeit money. They were so successful that counterfeiting is far less common than it used to be. Nevertheless, about $10 million in counterfeit money is made and passed into circulation each year.

Crime Lab 18: Identifying Counterfeit Money

Look carefully at some paper currency. Most counterfeit money comes as ten-, twenty-, and fifty-dollar bills. Examine a paper bill carefully with a hand lens. Notice how the portrait stands out from the background. Notice, too, how distinct are lines found in the hair. In a counterfeit bill the portrait tends to be more lifeless and merges with the background; the hair lines tend to be less distinct.

The many fine lines throughout a real bill are sharp and distinct; the numerals are clear, evenly spaced, and perfectly aligned. In counterfeit bills the lines are less sharp, and often the numbers are uneven or improperly aligned.

Counterfeiters often print red and blue lines on the paper to imitate the fine red and blue fibers found in real bills. Furthermore, the backs of counterfeit bills are often poor replicas of real bills. Counterfeiters tend to believe that people seldom look at the backs of their currency.

Take the time to look at paper currency closely. Talk to someone at a bank or to someone else who handles a lot of money on a daily basis. Such people are trained to recognize counterfeit money. They can give you some additional clues to look for. If you receive a bill that you think is counterfeit, ask a bank official to determine if it is. If so, then go to the police and tell them where you received the bill.

Codes

On January 17, 1917, Arthur Zimmermann, Germany's foreign minister, sent a coded message to Mexico promising the return of Mexico's "lost territories" of Texas, New Mexico, and Arizona if Mexico would declare war on the United States. The message was intercepted and decoded by British Intelligence, who forwarded their findings to President Woodrow Wilson. Wilson made the information public, and soon after the United States declared war on Germany.

During World War II, U.S. decoders intercepted and broke the code for Japanese naval messages in the Pacific. The information made it possible for

American forces to ambush a Japanese task force at Midway Island on June 14, 1942—thus turning the tide of the war in the Pacific. To prevent the Japanese from decoding U.S. military messages, the Marines sometimes used Navajo Indians, who communicated in their native language over radio. Their messages were never decoded.

Codes, which are systems of symbols used to transmit messages, have a great many uses. Coded messages often are meant to be secret. However, the best-known code, the Morse Code, is not secret. It consists of a series of dots and dashes used to represent letters. Originally it was used to transmit messages by telegraph. Similarly, scouts and the military often communicate with flags, which, held in different positions, can be used to represent different letters of the alphabet. Stores sometimes use codes in pricing items. The codes provide sales clerks with the price the store paid for an item. Knowing the original cost, the clerk will not sell items on sale at a price less than the cost to the store.

Following is a code that might be used to code prices. The letters in the word *surveying* could be used for the digits 1 to 9. The letter O could be used to represent zero (0). For example, a sweater might be labeled "$24.98 (SUVG)" to indicate that the cost to the company was $12.49. The sweater was marked up 100 percent. A suit might be labeled "$495.60 (REYNO)," indicating that its cost to the company was $356.80.

S	U	R	V	E	Y	I	N	G
1	2	3	4	5	6	7	8	9

Computers operate on a binary code called ASCII, which stands for American Standard Code for Information Exchange and is simply a number system that consists of two numbers, 0 and 1. If a switch is on, the number represented is 1. If the switch is off, the number represented is 0. Any number or letter can be represented by *1*s and *0*s. The following table shows the ASCII code for the numbers 1 to 9 and the letters *A, a, B, b, C,* and *c.*

Number or Letter	Binary Code	Number or Letter	Binary Code
0	0	8	1000
1	1	9	1001
2	10	A	1000001
3	11	a	1100001
4	100	B	1000010
5	101	b	1100010
6	110	C	1000011
7	111	c	1100011

Supermarkets use a bar code consisting of dark and transparent bars to represent *1*s and *0*s. You've probably seen a clerk at the checkout counter draw the bar code of a grocery item over a laser light. The laser beam reads the bar code as a series of binary numbers and feeds them to a computer, which converts them into a price that appears on the checkout display screen.

Crime Lab 101

During Prohibition, bootleggers used coded messages to communicate by radio about shipments, and some bookies still use codes to communicate with customers and other gamblers. Sometimes kidnappers use coded messages to communicate messages about ransom money.

If you have read Sherlock Holmes, you may be familiar with the code of the dancing men, which appeared in "The Adventure of the Dancing Men." In the story, a man reports that his wife, Elsie, became very upset when she received several notes containing a series of lines drawn to look like dancing men. Figure 20a shows three of the messages she received together with her one reply.

Holmes knew (as you might know from watching the TV show "Wheel of Fortune") that e is the most commonly used letter in the English language. If the most common letter in a coded message is *x*, then *x* probably represents e. Since the woman's name was Elsie, Holmes knew that he might expect to see her name as $E\_\_\_e$ within a message. He knew, too, the usage frequency of letters (from most frequent to least frequent) to be *e, t, a, o, n, i, r, s, h, d, l, u, c, m, p, f, y, w, g, b, v, j, k, q, x, z;* the most commonly paired letters to be *th, he, an, in, er, re, es,* and *on;* and a low-frequency letter that precedes a medium-frequency letter to always represent *qu*. He also knew that three rarely paired letters are *a, i,* and *o* and that the letter *h* follows verbs 80 percent of the time and precedes them 20 percent of the time.

Using his knowledge, some key assumptions, and a lot of thought, Holmes was able to decode the messages and establish a partial alphabet as shown in Figure 20b. Holmes decided that the little flags carried by some of the men indicated the end of a

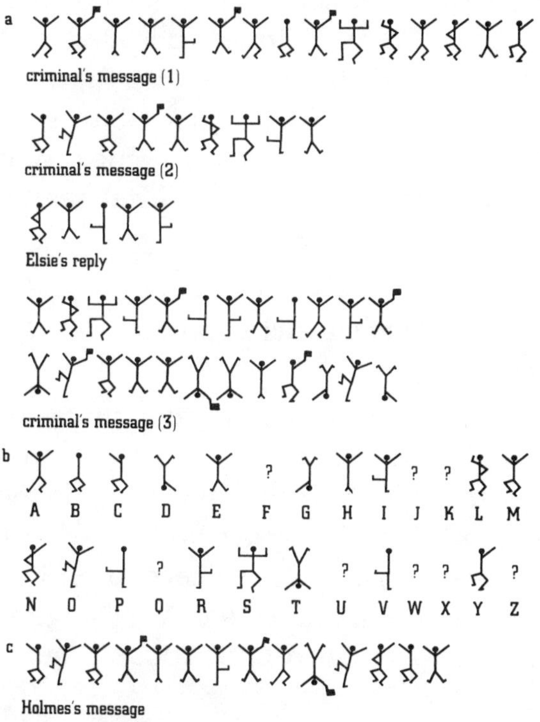

a
criminal's message (1)

criminal's message (2)

Elsie's reply

criminal's message (3)

b
A	B	C	D	E	F	G	H	I	J	K	L	M
						?			?		?	

N	O	P	Q	R	S	T	U	V	W	X	Y	Z
			?				?		?	?		?

c
Holmes's message

Figure 20   The dancing men used as a code in A. Conan Doyle's story "The Adventure of the Dancing Men." Sherlock Holmes figured out the code from his knowledge of the English language. He was able to read the messages (a) once he derived a portion of the alphabet (b). What do the messages say? Holmes trapped the criminal into coming to meet him by sending him the last message (c). What was Holmes's message?

word. The criminal, whose name was Abe Slaney, thought the code was known only to himself and Elsie. As a result, Holmes, who decided he had to act quickly after reading the criminal's third message, was able to trap the criminal by sending him a message written in code. The message is shown in Figure 20c. From Holmes's decoded alphabet (Figure 20b), see if you can decode the messages sent by the criminal, Elsie, and Holmes. Which message contains the criminal's name? Why did Holmes feel he had to act quickly after reading the criminal's third message?

Crime Lab 19: Sending and Breaking Coded Messages

Codes can be very complicated, but here are some simple codes that you can use to communicate with your friends. One code involves writing a message in zigzag fashion. The first letter appears on line 1, the second on line 2, the third on line 1, and so on. A message such as MEET ME AT THE CLUB HOUSE would be written:

M	E	M	A	T	E	L	B	O	S
E	T	E	T	H	C	U	H	U	E

Another approach is to substitute numbers for letters. You might, for example, number the letters in the alphabet from 1 to 26, substituting *1* for *a*, *2* for b . . . and 26 for z. Or you might choose a more complicated numbering system, using just three numbers, where $a = 111, b = 112$, c $= 113, d = 121 . . . z = 332$.

Entire messages might be written backward so that MEET ME AT THE CLUB HOUSE becomes ESUOH BULC EHT TA EM TEEM, or the letters might be shuffled in some prearranged order so that the message becomes EEMT EM TA HTE LUCB OUSHE. Another approach would be to use mirror writing. Leonardo da Vinci's notebook could be read only by holding it in front of a mirror.

Have a group of your friends divide into two or three small groups. Each group should devise a secret code that allows the members of the group to communicate with one another. Devising and using a code to communicate secret messages can be a lot of fun.

After all the groups have developed a code of their own, purposely "intercept" one another's codes and try to break them. Decoding is hard work if the code is a good one, so you might want to offer a prize to the group that first succeeds in decoding the messages of another group.

CODES AND CRIME

Criminals often find it necessary to communicate via or handle documents. They may be very careful not to leave fingerprints on the documents, but they can't avoid using a pen, typewriter, or some other device for writing their message. As you have seen, that writing device may leave clues of its own. Even if criminals communicate in code, they run the risk of their codes being decoded. Any code that can be devised can also be decoded, as you may have found in your own crime-lab work.

SIX

THE ART OF SLEUTHING

(A) detective reconstructing a crime is much like a scientist who uses all the facts to arrive at a hypothesis. The hypothesis should account for all the facts and suggest some other facts that have yet to be discovered. If the detective is a good one, he or she, like a good scientist, will keep an open mind about other hypotheses that might also explain the same set of facts.

SCIENCE AND CRIME DETECTION

Detectives must be able to use facts (the evidence) to piece together a consistent picture of a crime. They must separate the important evidence from the unimportant. This requires them to be skilled observers. They must see details, recognize the unexpected when it appears, and ask the right questions as they seek to find answers. From all the facts, they must be able to reason creatively so as to deduce a conclusion based on evidence.

Some fictional detectives, such as Sherlock Holmes or television's Lieutenant Columbo, are very good at this. For example, in one Sherlock Holmes story, Holmes turns to Watson and says, "I see that you've decided not to buy any South African securities."

"How in blazes do you know that?" responds Watson.

"Elementary, my dear Watson," replies Holmes, who then explains the sequence of events that led him to his deduction: (1) Watson had had chalk between his left thumb and fingers on the previous night after returning from his club. (2) He has chalk on his fingers only after playing billiards. (3) He plays billiards only with Mr. Thurston. (4) Watson had said a month before that Thurston had an option on some South African property that would expire in one month's time, and Thurston wanted Watson to invest money in the venture. (5) Watson's checkbook is in Holmes's locker, but Watson has not asked for the key. (6) The month is up. Watson had seen Thurston and had not paid him any money. Therefore, Watson must have decided not to invest in the South African scheme.

Watson then agrees that Holmes's argument is reasonable and based on elementary facts. But it's hard to believe that anyone would remember such a series of facts and observations while engaged in a variety of other activities. Real detectives don't have an author to create and remember the important clues as the story unfolds. They're stuck with a lot of facts that may seem totally unrelated.

Lieutenant Columbo uses a crime lab to evaluate

or analyze evidence in practically every episode and keeps a careful journal of facts, observations, and statements. Crime investigators generally make drawings of what they see and record the thoughts that occur to them as they try to make sense out of a jigsaw puzzle of clues. They also record things that need to be done, new hunches that need to be checked on the basis of additional evidence, and evidence that might be expected to turn up.

Good detectives must be able to think laterally as well as logically. Lateral thinkers have the ability to make associations between things normally seen as unrelated. Sometimes a good detective makes these associations when he or she is investigating a case unrelated to the associations that suddenly make sense. Sometimes these associations occur during a conversation or during sleep. Suddenly a relationship between facts is "seen" that was not recognized before. It may lead to an understanding of how or by whom the crime was committed.

CRIME DETECTION IS NOT ALWAYS SCIENTIFIC

In the Lindbergh kidnapping case, the police may *not* have proceeded in a scientific manner. They appear to have tried to make the evidence fit their hypothesis—Hauptmann is guilty—rather than develop hypotheses to fit the evidence. A taxi driver (Joe Perrone) had delivered a note to Dr. Condon, the contact between Lindbergh and the kidnappers. Perrone was given the note by a man who called himself John.

After Bruno Richard Hauptmann's arrest, Perrone was asked to identify Hauptmann, whom police believed to be John, the kidnapper. In such an identification, the suspect is placed in a lineup with a number of other people. The witness is then asked to pick out the suspect from the others. Just before he viewed the lineup, police told Perrone, "We've got the right guy. He matches the guy you described to us."

Perrone was then shown a lineup consisting of Hauptmann standing between two much larger policemen. Perrone quickly identified Hauptmann as John. On the other hand, Dr. Condon, who had talked with John at length, could not identify Hauptmann. He claimed Hauptmann had none of John's traits—light build, almond-shaped eyes, a fleshy lump at the base of his left thumb, and a husky voice—that he remembered. Condon's refusal to identify Hauptmann as the kidnapper infuriated the police, who wanted to wrap up the case quickly.

A failure to keep an open mind is one of the great mistakes police sometimes make. In 1990, Boston police, in an effort to solve a grisly case, were in such a hurry to arrest the slayer of a pregnant white woman that they wound up arresting the wrong person—who happened to be black. Despite inconclusive evidence and statistics that indicate a high level of violence inflicted by husbands on their wives, the police failed to consider the woman's husband a suspect.

Unfortunately, unscientific crime detection does not always arise from innocent oversights, incorrect tests, and similar errors. Instead, it can arise from official mismanagement of a case, sometimes deriving from things like racial bias and political pressures. This is precisely what happened in the Stuart case, in which Stuart "identified" his wife's killer for police. Luckily for the suspect, Stuart's brother, concerned that an innocent man might wind up in jail, came forth with the truth. Shortly thereafter, Stuart committed suicide. In a tragic way, in an already tragic chain of events that rocked the city of Boston for months, justice eventually was served.

BECOMING A BETTER OBSERVER

Some people, particularly fictional ones such as Sherlock Holmes, seem to be better observers than others, but all of us can improve our powers of observation through conscious effort and practice. By listening to a person talk, some observers can tell you the state or region, or even the city, where that person lives or is from. Detectives interviewing a suspect will make many observations as they ask questions. Is the suspect tall, short, fat, or thin? Does he or she wear a wedding ring? Are the hands callused or soft? How is the person dressed? Are the suspect's shoes large or small? Are they shined? Following are some activities that may help you to become a better observer.

Crime Lab Exercise 6: Making Careful Observations

O Carefully observe your living room, family room, or bedroom. What pictures hang in the room? What do they tell you about the interests of your family? What books or magazines do you find? What does the reading material tell you about the interests of your family? Are there clues about your family's religion? Are there hairs that indicate the presence of a dog or a cat? Are there ashes or ashtrays? Are there indications of a favorite color? What other observations can you make that provide information about your own family? What does the room tell you about your family or yourself?

Do the same thing when you visit a friend. If you have to sit in your dentist's or doctor's waiting room, see if you can figure out what his or her interests are.

O Sit silently in a room with a friend. Over a period of five minutes, each of you should record all the sounds you hear and all the odors you smell. After that period, exchange lists. Can you now hear some sounds that you missed before?

O Observe a friend for thirty seconds while he or she observes you. Then go into separate rooms and write down your observations. Your list might include hair color, eye color, how the hair is parted, visible scars, dimples, and so on.

List as many features as you can. Then come back together and exchange lists. Were any of your observations incorrect? Did you make any observations about your friend that he or she had never noticed before?

DEVELOPING IMAGINATION AND CREATIVE THINKING

Imagination and the ability to think creatively are important in solving crimes. They are also major goals of a good education. Solving problems in mathematics, writing stories, debating, considering how a different decision by a president or a congress might have changed the course of history, doing crossword puzzles, or designing an experiment to answer a question in science are all examples of ways in which education helps you to become more imaginative and creative. Following are some additional activities that may help you to further develop your thinking and thereby make you a better crime detector.

Crime Lab Exercise 7: Thinking Creatively

O Design, prepare, and play a board game or card game based on crime detection.

O Write a mystery using and extending what you have learned about crime detection.

O If you have a number of friends who enjoy sleuthing, as a group you might enjoy solving simulated (make-believe) crimes. At the scene of the mock murder, robbery, burglary, or whatever, provide some evidence—fingerprints, a note, hair, a footprint, a lip print, fibers from clothing, whatever seems appropriate. The person who sets up the crime and the evidence must have established a guilty party, that is, someone who will agree to provide the evidence. It might be a parent (a big footprint would lead sleuths to suspect an adult), a member of the group, a classmate, a friend, or a teacher. The sleuth group can then visit the scene of the crime, collect evidence, try to reconstruct the crime, and begin the search for the "criminal."

○ Collective thinking is often better than individual thinking. One form of collective thinking that can be fun and lead to imaginative solutions is called brainstorming. In a brainstorming session a question, issue, or puzzle is presented. Then members of a group offer ideas, suggestions, observations, or proposals leading to a consensus, solution, or solutions.

Brainstorming can be done as a crime-solving technique as well. Everyone in a small group could read a murder mystery up to the last chapter. The group could then get together and brainstorm about who is guilty. See if you can agree on who committed the crime and how the story will end. The magazine *Discover* has, or had, a section called "Brain Bogglers" in which readers were asked to read a one-page mystery and then solve the crime. (The answer is given on another page.) You might collect a series of these or similar mysteries and then brainstorm solutions with a group of friends or with your family.

THE DETECTIVE AS BLOODHOUND

One of the most boring parts of being a detective is following a suspect or tracking one down. Yet this is an important part of the profession. A prime suspect may have left town; he or she may have "jumped" bail. Someone may be strongly suspected of a crime, but there may not be enough evidence for an arrest. By watching the suspect closely, without being detected, the detective may find additional evidence. Or the person under surveillance may lead the detective to stolen goods, a missing body, or someone connected with the crime whom the police have been unable to locate.

In Chapter 4 you read about how John List, a missing murderer, was found by viewers who watched "America's Most Wanted" on television. Sometimes missing children are found when people recognize them from photographs on milk cartons or posters in post offices. Similarly, bank robbers may be recognized from faces seen on wanted posters. But not all missing persons are found.

In 1971, Jimmy Hoffa, the former Teamsters union president, was pardoned by President Richard Nixon after serving four years in prison. One of the stipulations in the pardon was that Hoffa not engage in union activities; yet, on July 30, 1975, he told his wife he was going to a meeting with Detroit Mafia boss "Tony Jack" Giacalone, former

Teamsters official "Tony Pro" Provenzano, and labor leader Leonard Schultz. At 2:30, Hoffa called his wife to tell her that none of the three had arrived for the meeting. She never heard from him again.

Giacalone, Provenzano, and Schultz all maintained that no meeting had been planned with Hoffa. Police followed various clues and anonymous tips in an effort to find him, but none of them produced Hoffa or his body. His disappearance remains a mystery.

On the evening of August 8, 1930, Joseph F. Crater, a newly appointed New York Supreme Court justice, bid his dinner companions farewell as he left for a 9:30 theater engagement. He was never seen again.

Although Crater was outwardly upright and true, he was a politician with ties to the infamous Tammany Hall. Just before he disappeared, he cashed checks for $5,100 and filled several briefcases with papers from his files. On January 31, 1931, his wife found a large envelope containing $6,690 in cash, three checks, stocks, bonds, three life insurance policies, a list of people who owed him money, and a letter signed "I am very *wary*. Joe." The police were baffled because they had searched the home thoroughly and had not found any such envelope. Nor did they ever learn what happened to Joseph Crater.

Some claimed that Crater had failed to make the $22,500 political payoff for his judgeship and was murdered. Others believed he had been killed because of some of his dealings with the underworld. Still others felt that he had fled to escape the irreversible corruption that had taken over his life. Was the money that his wife found placed there secretly by Crater after police had completed their investigation? We'll never know.

One of the strangest disappearances took place at sea. On December 4, 1872, the sailing ship *Mary Celeste* was sighted east of the Azores. The ship was without its captain, Benjamin Briggs, his wife, daughter, and seven crewmen. Various theories were developed to explain the abandoned ship, but none of them was ever confirmed.

Unlike a bloodhound who simply follows a scent, a detective must use his or her mind to find or follow a suspect. In the next two experiments you'll use your ingenuity in honing your "bloodhound" skills.

Crime Lab 20: Finding a Lost Person

Your first bloodhound duty will be easier than the work a detective might face. In fact, this job could be a lot of fun. Try to remember a friend or distant relative you knew several years ago who has moved away. You've lost track of that person. Your task is to find and talk to the "missing person." How will you proceed? Perhaps the school you both attended has sent records to another school. A mutual friend may be able to provide useful clues. If you can find the town or city to which the person has moved, look in a library for a telephone book for that place. What other methods can you think of that will help you find this missing person?

Crime Lab 21: Trailing a Suspect

Your next job involves following someone you know and may be more difficult than a similar job taken on by a detective. Usually a detective follows someone who doesn't know him or her. In fact, to avoid resentment and possible embarrassment, you'll need to make the task even more difficult. Tell a group of friends that sometime in the near future you're going to follow one of them for a day as part of your crime-detection training program. Assure them that you won't divulge the results of your observations to anyone else. If any of your friends objects to such surveillance, assure the person that you will not "put a tail" on him or her.

Like any good detective, you should probably form a team to trail your "suspect." Normally, to prevent someone being trailed from becoming suspicious, one detective will not follow the suspect continuously. A second, third, and even fourth detective will pick up the trail at a convenient time or place. Furthermore, the suspect should see the "detective" as little as possible. An unfamiliar face that keeps reappearing will make the person being followed suspicious.

After your team has followed your friend for a day or two, arrange to meet with your fellow "detectives." Put together an hour-by-hour record of your friend's locations for the time he or she was under surveillance.

PSYCHICS AND MISSING PERSONS

Some police departments make use of professed psychics or clairvoyants, people who claim to have an ability to perceive things beyond the range of our senses. A local New Jersey police department used a woman who claimed to have had a dream about a little boy caught in a pipe. When she went to the police several days later, they told her that a boy had fallen in the river and was believed to have drowned. However, the body had not been found. She agreed to use her "psychic" abilities to provide more information if possible. A psychiatrist placed her in a semi-hypnotic state, from which she reported seeing the number 8, a fence surrounding a school, a factory, and a gray house. When the body was finally found in a downstream pond, the investigator noticed that the pond was near Public School No. 8, which was enclosed by a fence. A gray house and a factory were also nearby. The investigator also found some large pipes in the stream leading to the pond. The boy's body may well have lain in one of the pipes before being washed into the pond. Furthermore, the boy's shoes were on the wrong feet, a detail that the psychic had reported.

In another case, a private detective asked the same woman to help him find a missing girl. The psychic said she could see the girl in an ill-kept house with a red door. On the door was a three-digit number with a 1 and a 6 in it. As she and the detective began driving the streets, the psychic said that they must look for something related to taxis on a street that had a president's name. On Monroe Street they found a house with number 186 that had an office that took calls for taxis. A woman in the office denied knowing anything about the missing girl, but the psychic maintained that the missing girl was there.

The next day, the girl's father asked the psychic to go with him to look for his daughter. The woman replied that she wanted to wait a day to avoid an accident. The father, together with the detective, decided not to wait. On their way to the address, their car was struck by another car. The next day, the bruised men accompanied the psychic to 186 Monroe Street, where they found the missing girl.

Many people do not believe that psychic powers exist. They say that psychics are like mind readers who perform on stage—entertaining and fun to watch but with no powers. Their so-called psychic powers are actually tricks similar to those performed by magicians.

Most mind readers who display their "powers" in public for pay will tell you that there are tricks to their trade. They can't really tell what anyone is thinking without tangible clues that they receive in one way or another. They would argue that the psychic described here had information that enabled her to lead police to the girl and to describe and locate the boy's body.

Others believe that some people do have psychic powers that cannot be explained scientifically. Some argue that all children less than six years of age have psychic powers but that only a few retain the power into adulthood. What do you think?

Crime Lab 22: Using "Psychic" Powers

This crime lab is possible only if you know someone who claims to have psychic powers. You might ask the psychic to help you locate something that you or one of your family have lost. Can he or she see the missing object and offer suggestions that will help you find it? If the psychic is willing, show him or her your watch or some other object that you plan to hide before meeting again at a later time. (Some psychics would not be willing to use their powers in this way.) Show it also to a friend who does not claim to have psychic powers. The friend will serve as a control in this experiment because it might be possible to find the missing article without any need for psychic powers. When you meet again, see if the psychic can offer insights or clues that would help your friend who served as the control in this experiment find the missing object.

THE ART OF QUESTIONING

One of a detective's jobs is to interview and question suspects, victims of crimes, and witnesses who were at the scene of the crime or who can verify alibis offered by suspects. This is not an easy task. You might think that two eyewitnesses to a crime would agree about what happened. But often their descriptions are very different. How do you know which person, if either, is telling the truth? People often are not objective. They tend to see and hear what they want to see and hear.

Police officers, too, are often not objective. They will seek a confession from a suspect who they are convinced is guilty, when in fact the suspect may be innocent. For example, in Canaan, Connecticut, in 1973 a woman named Barbara Gibbon was brutally murdered in her home. Her son, Peter Reilly, a high school student, claimed that he had returned in the evening to find his mother's bloody and beaten body.

State police called to the scene were convinced that Reilly had committed the crime. He was questioned for twenty-five hours, then allowed four hours' sleep before taking a lie detector test. After being told that he had failed the test and that perhaps he had committed the murder without being aware of what he was doing, Reilly confessed to the crime.

The Art of Sleuthing

At his trial, Reilly pleaded not guilty. Nevertheless, he was convicted on the basis of police testimony and his own earlier confession.

At a hearing prior to a second trial, a psychiatrist argued forcefully that the confession had been obtained by coercion. Later, Dennis Santore, who had replaced the former and by then deceased state's attorney, found in his predecessor's files evidence showing that Reilly could not have committed the crime—a number of people had seen him at least twenty miles from his home at the time of the crime. Based on the new evidence, Reilly was released.

If the police investigating Reilly had interviewed more people, they would have found that he was far from his home at the time of the crime. In a thorough investigation, the stories obtained from witnesses involved in or associated with a crime may differ considerably. In an effort to clarify those parts of the story where there is disagreement, police will often interview people several times. But unless the questions are well framed and thought out ahead of time, the time spent on such interviews may be wasted.

Watch a skilled interviewer like Mike Wallace on television. You'll find that Wallace knows as much about the topic being discussed as the person he's interviewing. Notice how he sometimes traps people who have changed their story during the interview. It's obvious that he has carefully prepared the questions he wants to ask.

Crime Lab 101

Here are some rules that may serve as a guide for questioning people:

① Begin by trying to put the person you are interviewing at ease. Ask questions and give responses that boost the person's ego. Lieutenant Columbo is so good at this that the person he is questioning often begins to feel superior to Columbo.

② Tell the person the purpose of the interview.

③ Long before the interview begins, think about what you want to learn from the person questioned. Then prepare your questions ahead of time so as to get the responses you want. Be sure that your questions cover all that you want to learn.

④ Try to keep the questions simple and direct. Don't ask a lot of questions that contain the word *and*. For example, don't ask, "Where were you on the night of January 22, *and* why were you there?" Find out where the person was and then ask why he or she was there.

If only one of several witnesses tells a story quite different from the others', you may suspect that that person is lying. In that case, you may want to look for inconsistencies in that person's story and try to catch him or her in an obvious lie. On the other hand, there may be as many stories as there are witnesses. It may be a matter of different people seeing and hearing different things. A double play in a professional baseball game is seen quite differently from the centerfield bleachers than from the pitcher's mound.

Crime Lab 23: Can You Believe What You Hear?

At a party with friends, or at a large family gathering, ask people to sit in a line or circle. You will whisper to one person a message that you have written on a sheet of paper. That person will whisper what you said to the next person, and so on until the message has passed all the way around the circle or along the entire line. At that point, ask the last person to receive the message to tell you what he or she heard.

The message that you whisper first might be something like, "If the sun rises in the morning, need the moon set at night?" or "The price of a democracy is the eternal vigilance of its citizens." How does the message you whispered compare with the message spoken by the last person? Do you see why a good trial judge does not allow hearsay evidence?

Almost every day someone tells you a story that makes you wonder, "Is that really true?" When you encounter such a story, one that you think you can safely investigate, go ahead and begin your questioning. Question people who may have seen or been present at the event. Just what *did* take place? Question as many people as possible. Do their stories agree? If not, is there some way to find out who is telling the truth? Possibly, everyone is telling the truth. What they saw depends on where and/or how they saw or heard the event. Some people may have seen or heard something that other people missed because they were too far away or at the wrong angle, or for some other reason.

The following crime-lab exercises will help you to understand that there are often flaws in the way we perceive the things we see.

Crime Lab Exercise 8: Seeing Is Not Necessarily Believing

O Draw a horizontal straight line about a foot long on a blackboard or a large sheet of paper hanging on a wall. Then ask a person to draw a vertical line that appears to be the same length above or beside the horizontal line. Measure the two lines with a ruler. Which line is longer? Does it look longer? Try this same experiment several times with different people. Are the results always the same?

O Look at the drawings in Figure 21 and answer the question accompanying each drawing. Then make measurements to test your answers. What do you find? Can you always believe what you see?

O Look at a car in a parking lot illuminated by sodium vapor lamps. What color do you think the car is? Then look at the same car in sunlight or ordinary white light. What color is it now?

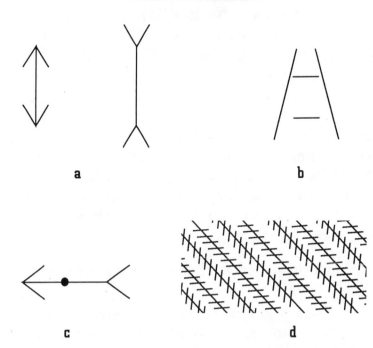

a   b

c   d

Figure 21   Can you always believe what you see? (a) Which
of the two vertical lines is longer? (b) Which of the two
horizontal lines is longer? (c) Is the horizontal line to the left of
the circle equal in length to the line to the right of the circle?
(d) Are the long diagonal lines parallel?

○ Replace the bulb in your bedroom light
with a green light bulb. At night, turn off all
other lights except the green bulb. Look at an
object you know to be red in the green light.
What color does it appear to be? What will a
blue object look like in green light? A yellow
object? A white object? How about a green
object?

Crime Lab 101

INTERVIEWING WITNESSES

Much of a crime detector's time is spent interviewing witnesses or suspects. If everyone told the truth and agreed on what he or she saw, a crime detector could leave an interview feeling confident that what was said was true. However, some people do tell lies. And some witnesses who really believe they're telling the truth relate stories different from those told by equally well-intentioned observers.

The next crime lab will help you understand the problems a detective might face in interviewing witnesses to a crime.

Crime Lab 24: Can You Believe What People Say They Saw?

○ Show a group of people a colored picture. A photograph or a painting from a book is fine as long as it contains a number of people and objects. That is, the picture should be reasonably complicated, like the scenes we view every day. Choose one that you think will be interesting and has specific information in it, such as a calendar with a date, a dog or cat of a well-known breed, or people of different races. If you can't find such a picture, draw one of your own. Pass the picture around and give everyone a few seconds to look at it. Then ask each person to write down what he or she saw in the picture.

○ Collect the comments and compare them. What did most people notice? Did any of them claim to see things that weren't in the picture? Ask them some specific questions about the picture—for example, "What was the date on the calendar?" "What kind of animal was in the picture?" "Can you describe the animal?" "What was the color of the rug?"

How many mistakes did they make? On how many details do they disagree?

O Ask someone ahead of time to come into a party or a family gathering at your home and commit a "crime." (Be sure to obtain your parents' permission before you do this so that they don't interfere with the "intruder.") Choose someone who is unknown to everyone except you and your parents. The person should simply walk into the house without knocking, pass through the people, go to your room, take several books from your desk or shelves, and carry them back through the gathering and out the door. If anyone stops the intruder, the intruder can say that the books are being borrowed with your permission for a school project. You should plan to be out of sight during the time that this "crime" is being committed.

O At some point after the crime, ask a number of different "witnesses" in separate interviews to describe the intruder and tell what the intruder did. How do their observations compare? How do they compare with what the intruder actually did? Did the witnesses notice what the intruder was wearing? Can they accurately describe the length and color of his or her hair? Did they correctly observe the intruder's eye color? Height? Weight? Facial features?

Detectives usually ask a number of eyewitnesses to relate what went on at the scene of a crime and to describe the criminal. Do you think the witnesses will provide them with detailed descriptions and accounts that will agree closely with one another?

IDENTIFYING VOICES

In the Lindbergh case, you will remember from the beginning of this chapter, Dr. Condon was unable to identify the police's prime suspect, Bruno Richard Hauptmann, as John—the kidnapper he had talked to. At the trial, however, Dr. Condon did identify Hauptmann as John. His identification came after Colonel Lindbergh claimed Hauptmann's voice to be that of a man who had called out two words—"Hey Doc!"—from a hiding place as Lindbergh waited for Condon in a car nearby. Many believe that Dr. Condon's admiration of Lindbergh was so strong that he believed the colonel to be infallible. Even though two years had passed since Lindbergh had heard those two words, once Lindbergh identified Hauptmann as John, Condon decided that Hauptmann must be the guilty party.

Do you think a witness could positively identify

someone from his or her voice alone? To find out, try the next Crime Lab.

Crime Lab 25: Identifying a Person's Voice

Gather a group of friends, classmates, or family members in one room. If possible, try to include some people you haven't known for very long. Stand outside the room where you can't see them. Ask them to choose one person who in his or her own voice will say just two words: "Hey Doc!"

After the person has said, "Hey Doc!" come back into the room and ask *each person* to say, "Hey Doc!" Can you identify the person who spoke by hearing just those two words?

Repeat this experiment a number of times. How many of the people in the group can you identify in this way? They should choose to speak in a random order with some people repeating so that you can't guess later ones by eliminating those who have already spoken.

After you've had a try, perhaps some of your "colleagues" would like to test their skill at identifying voices. Based on a number of trials, what do you think about evidence based on witnesses who say they recognized a suspect's voice? Does it seem to make a difference if the voice is a familiar one as opposed to the voice of someone you have met only recently?

If possible, repeat this experiment with a group of people you don't know. A teacher might let you use a classroom of students in a different grade or even at a different school. Or, if you don't know the guests very well, you might try it, with permission, at a sibling's party held in your home. Is voice identification more difficult if you don't know the speakers?

It might also be interesting to try the same experiment using voices transmitted by telephone. It might be fun to see if someone you know very well can change his or her voice so that you don't recognize it over the telephone. As you probably know, some people are quite good at imitating the voices of others. If you know someone with such an ability, see if that person can convince you that he or she is someone else on the telephone.

From what you have learned, do you think it likely that Lindbergh could have positively identified Hauptmann based on having heard him speak two words several years prior to the trial? If you had been a member of the jury, would Lindbergh's identification of Hauptmann have convinced you that he was guilty?

SEVEN

USING YOUR CRIME-DETECTING SKILLS

(T) hroughout this book you've had a chance to develop, hone, and practice your crime-detecting skills. Now it's time to begin seeking and solving your own cases. Some suggestions to get you started on "crimes" that you might investigate around your home and school are given here. The list contains just a few of the "mysteries" you might pursue. Once you begin, you'll probably find so many other "crimes" to investigate that you'll have a full load of cases all the time.

CASES TO SOLVE IN YOUR HOME OR SCHOOL

You can use your crime lab and practice your "crime"-detecting skills by solving some of the "cases" that occur in your own home or school. A few of the cases that you might investigate are listed here. With a little thought and imagination, it's likely that you'll find so many unsolved cases that you won't have time to solve all of them. You may have to take on an associate to keep up with your caseload.

Crime Lab 101

○ Who drank from the glass found on the kitchen counter? You may need to consult your file of lip prints to solve this one!

○ Did someone use your comb or hairbrush? If so, who was it?

○ Who squeezed the toothpaste tube in the middle?

○ Who opened the refrigerator after dinner?

○ Who wrote the note on the kitchen or refrigerator door? What pen was used to write it?

○ Is the story about your classmate true?

○ Was it a cat, a dog, or a human who left hairs on the living room couch?

○ From a careful analysis of crumbs, determine what your little brother or sister had for lunch. Or determine what your family had for dinner when you were out.

○ Who left the basement light on?

○ Who took a bite out of an apple and then left it on the kitchen table?

○ Where do you find litter around the grounds of your home or school? Develop a hypothesis to explain why it is where you find it and who the guilty litterbugs are. Then use surveillance to check your hypothesis.

A snowstorm, even a light snowfall, will allow you to solve some of the following mysteries.

○ Where does your cat or dog go when you let him or her outside?

Using Your Crime-Detecting Skills

○ Who was the last person to come into your house?

○ What cars or trucks came into your driveway during the afternoon or evening? Which vehicle was the last one to enter or leave?

○ What kinds of animals walked across your yard during the night?

As you go on solving "crimes," consider what you read at the beginning of Chapter 6: A good detective, like a good scientist, will keep an open mind. You may have a hypothesis that explains all the facts, but remember, there may be another hypothesis that explains them even better. Don't mistake suspicion for guilt. In the United States any suspect is innocent until *proven* guilty.

FOR FURTHER READING

Adams, Barbara Johnston. *Crime Mysteries*. New York: Watts, 1988.

Berger, Gilda, and Melvin Berger. *Bizarre Crimes*. New York: Messner, 1985.

Doyle, A. C. *The Complete Sherlock Holmes*. New York: Doubleday, 2 vol., 1960.

Fisher, James. *The Lindbergh Case*. New Brunswick, N.J.: Rutgers University Press, 1987.

Gardner, Robert. *Experimenting with Illusions*. New York: Watts, 1990.

Gustafson, Anita. *Guilty or Innocent*. New York: Holt, 1985.

Haskins, James. *Street Gangs: Yesterday and Today*. New York: Hastings, 1974.

Kennedy, Ludovic. *The Airman and the Carpenter*. New York: Viking, 1985.

Lewis, Alfred Allan. *The Evidence Never Lies*. New York: Holt, 1984.

Loeb, Robert. *Crime and Capital Punishment*. New York: Watts, 1978.

Madison, Arnold. *Arson*. New York: Watts, 1978.

———. *Great Unsolved Cases*. New York: Watts, 1978.

For Further Reading

————. *Vandalism: The Not-So-Senseless Crime.* Boston: Houghton Mifflin, 1981.

Mysteries of the Unexplained. Pleasantville, N.Y.: The Reader's Digest Association, 1990.

Paige, David. *A Day in the Life of a Police Detective.* Tulsa, Okla.: EDC Publishing, 1982.

Rawlins, David, and Bruce Rawlins. *Protect Yourself Against Crime: Defense Is Your Best Offense.* Tampa, Fla.: Axelrod, 1989.

Solomon, Louis. *The Ma and Pa Murders and Other Perfect Crimes.* New York: Lippincott, 1977.

Zonderman, Jon. *Beyond the Crime Lab: The New Science of Investigation.* New York: Wiley, 1990.

INDEX

Index

Index